CRISIS
IN
COMMUNICATION

CRISIS IN COMMUNICATION

A Christian Examination of the Mass Media by

MALCOLM BOYD

Doubleday & Company, Inc., Garden City, New York, 1957.

Printed in the United States of America
Library of Congress Catalog Card Number: 57-5781
Designed by Diana Klemin

To Beatrice Boyd

ACKNOWLEDGMENTS

I should like to thank the persons who painstakingly read the first completed draft of the book and whose criticisms were most helpful in the process of reorganizing and rewriting: Sherman E. Johnson, Janet Lacey, Michael B. Foster, Horton W. Davies, Hendrik Kraemer, Robert S. Paul and Dewi Morgan. The encouragement and counsel of Theodore O. Wedel of the College of Preachers and John Bachman of the Union Theological Seminary have proven to be of inestimable value.

My thanks are offered to the following persons and institutions: the Rt. Rev. Francis Eric Bloy, Bishop of the Diocese of Los Angeles, for his enduring understanding and guidance; the Church Divinity School of the Pacific and the Union Theological Seminary, and particularly Robert N. Rodenmayer and Paul E. Scherer of the respective seminaries, for theological education and Christian nurture; Reinhold Niebuhr, as much for the example of his patience and quiet humility as for the vigor and value of his ideas; the Ecumenical Institute of the World Council of Churches, Château de Bossey, Switzerland, for theological stimulus and Christian fellowship, and also for asking me to lecture about mass media at the 1955 Course for Theological Students; the Department of Inter-Church Aid and Refugee

Service of the British Council of Churches, for enabling me to study at first hand several of the experiments in Christian communication mentioned in this book; Pusey House, Oxford, for hospitality which I gratefully received there; Mary Pickford, Charles "Buddy" Rogers, Dale Evans, Roy Rogers, James K. Friedrich and Harry Wayne McMahan, for their sustained support and encouragement; Carol Murphy, for technical assistance in the writing of this book; the library staff of the Academy of Motion Picture Arts and Sciences, in Hollywood, for research advice and assistance; *Episcopal Churchnews,* for providing an initial outlet for my views about mass media. Gratitude is expressed to the following publications for permission to use, in this book, material contained in various of my published articles: *The Christian Century, Christianity and Crisis, Motive, Anglican Theological Review, Religion in Life, Union Seminary Quarterly Review, The Hollywood Reporter, Variety* and *Episcopal Churchnews.*

There are various persons whom I should like to thank individually. Without their vision, stimulus and friendship, this book would not have been written. They live in such scattered places as London, Denver, São Paulo, Athens, Oxford, Berkeley, Istanbul, Geneva, Los Angeles, Paris, San Francisco and New York. They will identify themselves and, I trust, accept my appreciation.

Thanks be to God.

Malcolm Boyd

PREFACE

Our age is receiving many descriptive labels. One of the most recent on the scene is the slogan "The Age of Publicity." Radio, television, the movies and the paper-back bookstall have opened channels for mass communication unknown to our grandfathers. The evangelist of the Christian gospel shares with the advertiser of lipstick or refrigerators the problem of how these communication techniques can best be put to use. Are they opportunity for the Church or dangerous competition? What are the limits of effectiveness of a radio sermon, for example—a monologue listened to by isolated individuals out of contact with a worshiping fellowship? Can a "religious" movie ever fully avoid the danger of sentimental pietism or that of exploiting the realism of a biblical story (that of Samson and Delilah, for instance) for purely sensational effects? Or is Church evangelism on better ground when it asks of mass communication nothing more than loyalty to truth, however secular may be the subject matter with which it deals by way of content? The Gospel could then enter upon an honest dialogue with the world portrayed in secular art or news story.

These and other issues receive wise analysis in Malcolm Boyd's book. The author, an honored former citizen of Hollywood and long at home in radio, motion-picture and television studios, has become a clergyman in the Episcopal Church and is also the recent recipient of a postgraduate degree in Theology at Union Theological Seminary in New York. He is thus uniquely equipped to deal with the subject of mass communication and its relevance in the life of the contemporary Church.

Theodore O. Wedel
College of Preachers
Washington, D. C.

CONTENTS

CRISIS
IN
COMMUNICATION

THE AGE OF PUBLICITY

INTRODUCTION We live and move and have our being in the Age of Publicity. The French sociologist, André Siegfried, refers to "l'age de la publicité" in his booklet *Aspects du XXme siècle.* The American critic, Louis Kronenberger, who says that "perhaps, our age is more than anything else the Age of Publicity," sees "the two key figures of the age" as being the press agent and the psychoanalyst. He has written that, in terms of affecting our lives today, "the only man fit to be compared with Sigmund Freud or Karl Marx is P. T. Barnum."[1] Mr. Barnum, the king of circus enterprises, relied heavily upon a barrage of publicity, stunts, sensational gimmicks and unhampered tub-thumping.

A number of other, and varied, observers of the contemporary scene have noted the same phenomenon. The news commentator, Eric Sevaried, pointed out that we worship "publicity gods." Clare Boothe Luce had this to say about Pope Pius XII: "If there could be such a thing in this modern age as a Saint of Public Relations, he is this

Pope."[2] *Time,* speaking of Billy Graham, wrote: "While Evangelist Graham sincerely considers himself nothing but a tool of God, he believes in giving God plenty of help with some tools of his own. The tools he has fashioned add up to an intricate technology of soul-saving that might astonish St. Paul, bewilder John Wesley and give any Madison Avenue adman some ideas."[3] We Christians have not even begun to plumb the depth of our involvement with the mass media. Unbelievable naïveté best describes our reaction to the robot-like techniques and gadgets that are pushing our lives around—and no one's life is excepted. I am often reminded of the little girl whose family carefully protected her from any knowledge of television, even to removing the TV program listing from the daily paper, but who appeared before me dressed in a complete Hopalong Cassidy outfit! So little does ignorance or disdain protect us from involvement in the age of publicity.

Let us examine this power of publicity in the light of Christian theology and Christian involvement. First, let us make clear a distinction between publicity and public relations.

Publicity is a spotlight. The outlet and the fruition of publicity is news. In fact, publicity *is* publicity by virtue of its being channeled, or having an outlet, or being itself publicized. Publicity, when effectively channeled through such outlets as newspapers, magazines, films, television or radio, builds reputations of individuals and institutions. Ironically, however, publicity may be harmful and, in fact, destroy the reputation of individuals and institutions.

Publicity is only a part of public relations. Public relations is, essentially, the climate of relationship and understanding between an individual and an institution, or between individuals, or between institutions. Public relations is a process in action whenever any institution exists in a community, or any two persons start talking to one another on a bus. Public relations—human relations; there is actually very little difference between them, only the difference we allow there. Good public relations may call for the total lack of any publicity, as, for example, when publicity in mass media will create a false picture of an individual or institution.

THE CHURCH'S EVANGELICAL CHALLENGE

St. Paul was a great public relations man for the Christian faith. He was not only a press agent and a publicity man; he was fully a public relations man. The distinction, as we have seen, is important. Every Christian is called upon to be a public relations man or woman for the Christian faith. God was in Christ reconciling the world unto Himself. That work of reconciliation, fully accomplished for us by Jesus Christ, the Son of God, has yet to be completed in us. This completion is actively carried on by God the Holy Spirit, who works in, and through, Christians as instruments of His work.

As Christians, we seek to obey the command of Christ to the disciples (Mark 16:15): "Go ye into all the world, and preach the Gospel to every creature." The Christian faith is not something to be clutched possessively, or to be used selfishly. If a man decides to "use" the faith in such a manner, he finds to his chagrin that what he is clutching possessively or using selfishly is not the faith. Evangelism is a part of the very faith of the Church.[4] A report from the Second Assembly of the World Council of Churches sharply reminds us:

The people of God are in this world as the Church, and they are never alone with their Lord in isolation from the world. It is the world *which He came to save. Without the Gospel the world is without sense, but without the world the Gospel is without reality. Evangelism is no specialized or separable or periodic activity, but is rather a dimension of the total activity of the Church. Everything the Church does is of evangelizing significance. Through all the aspects of its life the Church participates in Christ's mission to the world, both partaking of the Gospel and seeking to communicate it. Evangelism is the place where the Church discovers itself in its true depth and outreach.*[5]

If we as Christians do not accept the Church's mission to the world, we tend to move dangerously close toward the heresy of *dichotomization* in the great, one world of Almighty God. One is unable to limit the sovereignty of God to one area of life and to deny His total involvement in another area of life. Dichotomization, in fact, occurs when we make "Religion" a department of life. Religion then takes its place along with other departments of life; each is autonomous, and life is cut up into neat, perhaps exactly even, slices. Here, we shall place the Theatre; there, we shall place History; over here, in this neat little stack, we shall place Television; there, in that pile, over there in the corner, we shall place Books. Are we not buffoons, and, at the same time, tragedians, when we indulge in this game of slicing up the universe?

Our newspapers and magazines treat "Religion" as a "department" in the news. Occasionally, in instances such as the World Council of Churches assembly at Evanston, or the grave illness of the Pope, or the coronation of the Queen of England by the Archbishop of Canterbury, "Religion" hops out of its department and lands on the front page. Frequently, of course, "Religion" on the front page is located under a headline about controversy of some kind: the inability of delegates to a conference to agree about receiving Holy Communion together, or the fight raging among churchmen as to who will be elected to what. A front-page "Religious" spectacle in the United States not long ago concerned a priest who was locked out of a church building and who then broke the locks and entered, with the result that the congregation witnessed the historic scene of two clergymen conducting services simultaneously and in competition with one another. In a case such as this, "Religion" is hot news.

It is not the "Religion" pages of the newspapers, and the "Religion" sections of the news magazines, that have segregated "Religion" from the whole of life, making it into a mere section of life. The churches have done this. They have achieved this by not seeing clearly and proclaiming seriously God's involvement in, and sovereignty over, every area of life.

God is holy. God is all-powerful. God is possessed of all knowledge. God is present everywhere. ". . . if I go down to hell, thou art there also."

God the Holy Spirit is at work in the sanctuary of a church building; He is present and at work also in the hospital sickroom, in the giant newspaper city-desk slot, in church organization headquarters, in the hot television studios and in the hearts of all the men and women who are in all of these places. Whether in the sanctuary or in the newspaper office, men may deny His presence and oppose His power, but He is nevertheless there.

Quite frequently in the Church one encounters an unmistakable self-consciousness about public relations. Isn't it "brassy"? Isn't it "new" and "unconventional"? Wouldn't it be better just to go along, quietly and conservatively? "Why should we bring the public into this at all?"

In my opinion, this is directly akin to the repudiation of means of medical aid on the basis of avowed religious grounds.

Surely God, who is present always in each part of His creation, is present in the means to alleviate the sufferings and sicknesses of mankind, mental and physical. As God is sovereign over the "world" of medicine and healing, and is present in the implements of that "world" as in the implements of the whole world, so God is present in the methods of public relations, of disseminating His Word (and all words) to mankind. God is sovereign over the "world" of public relations as over the whole world. (It is to be understood that this implies no negation of demonic influences.)

I place in quotes "world" as applied to medicine and public relations. Men have become specialists and tend to see the world in the light of their own "world" of intensified interests. One of the basic things for all men, inside and outside the Church, is to see that God is sovereign over *one world* and that all its component parts are made one in, and through, Him.

The *Benedicite* comes to mind in this connection. It opens: "O all ye Works of the Lord, bless ye the Lord: praise him, and magnify him for ever." If a modern were composing a twentieth-century counterpart of the *Benedicite,* he might well write as follows: "O ye Television, Press, Films and Radio, bless ye the Lord: praise him, and magnify him for ever."

Public relations, then, is not an isolated "world" that is radically removed from the Church. The Church, like the effective public relations office, must know the pulse of the world if it is to minister effectively to men. The Sacraments are to be administered to all men. How may men know about them and seek them if they are shut up inside a guarded temple and not held high for all the world to behold? The Word of God is to be preached to the ends of the earth. What follows from this?

We cannot say that we are exalting the Name of God if we fearfully run away, without faith, from a new instrument or technique that He may guide us to use for His glory. We are not exalting the Name of God if we become clannish and exclusive to the point where we do not even use media that are a part of God's world, whereby His Word may be spread more effectively to men in desperate need of it. We are not exalting the Name of God if we try to segregate Him from the "world" of newspapers, magazines, radio, TV and the motion picture. God's knowledge and sovereignty extend as much to TV script conferences and newspaper editorial rooms as to Young People's Fellowship suppers and Every-Member canvasses. The Body of our Lord, and His Blood, preserve unto everlasting life the bodies and souls of clergymen and actors, parish secretaries and news photographers.

The words "public relations" are sometimes smugly used within the Church to imply that we, as churchmen, are somehow better than, and above, the purveyors of publicity. Yet if we are not the purveyors of the Good News and public relations agents for the Kingdom of God, what are we? This applies to all ministers and to all laymen. The activity of St. Paul as a purveyor of the Word and public relations man for Jesus Christ gives to the field the highest possible stature. I note with considerable interest Abbé Michonneau's reference to the speculation that if St. Paul were to come back to our world in the flesh, he would become a newspaperman. He would, as public relations man or newsman, be using all possible God-given methods and tools to communicate God's Word to all people. Of course, this is exactly what St. Paul, as public relations man and newsman, *did* in his ministry. The Rev. Dr. Clayton T. Griswold told a conference: "For the Church (of today) not to make extensive use of radio and television would be as unthinkable as if St. Paul refused to travel in ships or Luther and Calvin had looked down on the printing press as unworthy of their use.[6]

The Holiness of God is found, not diffused but whole in essence, in all areas of life. This does not contradict the awesome sense of the Numinous. For, in isolating or defining the sense of the Numinous, one is blasphemously limiting it. God the Father Almighty, Creator of heaven and earth, is the Lord of cinema, television-radio, medicine, sports, people, foreign affairs, books—as well as of life, death and resurrection. The Church, as the Body of Christ, is not an isolated part of life but is involved in all the wholeness and fullness of life.

The Church in the Age of Publicity is confronted by nothing quite so simple as a choice between "use" and "nonuse" of the media of mass communication. We cannot be simply "for" or "against" mass media. We *find* that we must come to grips with the acute problem of "correct use" and "misuse."

The end does not justify any means that are not in accordance with it. The true end of publicity is to *communicate* in a lucid, straightforward, simple way. It is therefore a misinterpretation of public relations and a misuse of publicity to promote titillating exposure—which, at its worst, lays claim upon "morality" and can be quite self-righteous—or exploitation, perversion of truth into fraction-truth, keyhole-peeping sensation and falsehood.

The average person's present-day desire to know the truth about other persons, places and things is inherently a healthy desire. A magazine profile on Sylvester L. Weaver (former National Broadcasting Company executive) captured his vivid way of regarding communication. It noted:

While other men at N.B.C. usually refer to radio and television simply as "radio-TV," Weaver is likely to call them "electronic communications into the home." To Weaver, the room in which N.B.C. news is assembled and broadcast is not merely a newsroom; it is a communications center. And a man who presides over a news program is not a newscaster; he is a communicator. The concept of the communicator, connoting, as it does for Weaver, the powerful resources of thought, technology, showmanship, and cultural enlightenment, is one that he especially delights in, and, as president of N.B.C., with all its sprawling facilities, he is inclined to see himself in the role of a super-communicator, gathering high-level intelligence from everywhere, pondering its complexities, making decisions, informing the people, and influencing the shape to come.[7]

Mr. Weaver's emphasis upon "communications" and "communicator" is healthy. It can teach us something as Christians. Surely, a Christian is by the sheer fact of his baptism called to be a communicator. As a Christian, he cannot help but be involved in communicating the saving Gospel of God in Christ. Just as surely, the Church is a communications center of salvation. A noncommunicating Church would be a contradiction in terms.

The immense power of publicity and its pressure upon life today points up, for the Christian, a paradox in which he finds himself. *It is the difficult task of the Church both to employ the implements and techniques of public relations and publicity in doing its missionary work—and, as a part of its mission in the world, to stand in judgment upon these implements and techniques.*

We cannot avoid the challenge and implications of this problem.

The tension between use of present-day techniques and implements and the necessity to stand in judgment upon them represents a major challenge to the thought and work of the Church. It is my faith that the Church can use these tools of public relations creatively, as well as criticize them in the light of the divine judgment under which the Church must also stand.

THE WEAPON OF EXPLOITATION

We must now face the worst of what the misuse of these powerful mass media is doing and can do.

At the outset, it must be understood that there are no basically new forces in the world. Rather, there is an accentuation of the influence and power of basic forces that have always been at work in the world. Man himself remains the same, as having been created in the image of God, as having "fallen" and as a sinner. To exploit is an easier thing for him to do than to love. He has always, since the mythical Fall, sinned and exploited. He has reigned in a fake kind of majesty at the core of his egocentric being. He has gloried, whatever the historical period, in usurping the functions of divinity, in "playing God." Today the technological process has insanely afforded man new and absurdly powerful push buttons to play with, new machines that appear to annihilate distances between places and persons, new techniques insisting on such closeness that individuality may be destroyed.

We live in a technical society. Encased within our culture are institutions that nourish and control media of mass communication. These institutions require our sharp awareness and studied action. Of themselves, the mass media are neutral. Harnessed, however, to serve man and to fulfill our self-centered, exploitation-directed will for them, these media possess potential for great harm. Needless to say, they possess also potential for great good. Television or the press is, in this regard, similar to nuclear energy, church-building projects or our own minds and bodies. By the misuse of the media of mass communication, however, some of us have sharpened and refined the machinery of exploitation.

Foreseeing, with remarkable astuteness, what lay ahead, Sören Kierkegaard wrote, as long ago as 1851:

> *Indeed, the apogee has almost been attained: communication has just about reached the lowest point, with respect to its importance; and contemporaneously the means of communication have pretty nearly attained the highest point, with respect to quick and overwhelming distribution. For what is in such haste to get out, and on the other hand what has such widespread distribution as . . . twaddle? Oh, procure silence!* [8]

Many persons cry out today the same words: procure silence! Others, desiring to harness the power of the mass media for Christian evangelization, take an opposite stand. Procure silence we cannot. New sounds, blatant sounds, sounds wheedling us and tempting us and screaming at us, are abroad in the world. These sounds demand a response. God has given us free wills, to Him we are not robots; but these demonic sounds abroad in the world (the cry of the huckster, the shout of the totalitarian dictator using mass techniques) are directed to us as robots. To the men behind the sounds, making the sounds, we are potentially robots. A free response from us as individuals is sought only in respect to our place within a mass, and our being moved as a part of that mass.

We are losing, in ways sometimes subtle and sometimes very obvious, our identity as "persons" in this technical age of overpowering changes and tensions. A British observer has noted:

We find out how our neighbors think by consulting the results of the Gallup Poll. Our ideas, like our food, come individually wrapped, and sterilized.[9]

The influence of films has long been recognized. This is the fullness of time when trade follows the film, when thought and action patterns are moulded by celluloid styles. All films are "message" films. The impact of the press and of radio is well documented. And now, the newer, stronger impact of television is being experienced.

We cannot disengage ourselves, as Christians, from the mass media themselves or from the problems with which they challenge us. This is true for two main reasons. First, our missionary imperative commands us to preach the Gospel to all men. How can we, in the face of our Lord's will, refuse to use such potentially vital methods as mass media in reaching out with God's Word to desperately isolated men and women? Secondly, it is increasingly becoming obvious that we are being evangelized by our secular technical society far more than we are in the process of evangelizing it for Jesus Christ. The Church's manifest task is to evangelize this society and age and condition. F. D. Maurice speaks in a telling way to our ever fresh inclination to run away from the dynamic challenges of the world:

Must I utterly renounce all the things about me, that I may be absorbed into Him, or is there any way in which I can devote them and myself to Him, and only know Him the better by filling my place among them?[10]

Assuming our Christian involvement with the mass media, we cannot help examining the factor of motivation. Are there some techniques we must reject, and, regarding them, speak prophetically to society? Are we ever to "exploit" for Christ? Of course, as we are sinners and enmeshed in complex personal and institutional ambiguities, we shall exploit for Him. But are we to *seek* to exploit for Him? Are we to make a conscious evangelical effort to exploit for Him?

Dr. Billy Graham was quoted in an interview in *The Observer:* "I am selling the greatest product in the world: why shouldn't it be promoted as well as soap?"[11] In an American magazine article, Dr. Graham has elaborated upon this point:

In every other area of life, we take for granted publicity, bigness, modern techniques. Why should not the church employ some of these methods, that are used by big business or labor unions to promote their products or causes, in order to win men for Christ?[12]

It is true: we live in the Age of Publicity. We certainly take publicity for granted. We have little choice, living as we do in this technical age, this competitive, mass-media-marked, hopped-up society. A world-wide audience of 145,800,000 persons *weekly* views Hollywood motion pictures, it is reported by the 1956 *Film Daily Year Book.* The Columbia Broadcasting System tells us, in an advertisement in *Variety* (July 25, 1956):

NOBODY'S LISTENING BUT PEOPLE—*ALL OF THEM STEADY EATERS! What a time to talk about food—while* 4,115,000 people a minute *are listening attentively to daytime CBS radio. Mostly they're homemakers, too busy for other advertising media. They're listening to 11 serial dramas on CBS Radio, starting at 12:00 noon, CNYT, Monday through Friday. In one week, these programs reach* 20,548,000 different people.

Advertising Research Foundation counted 37,277,000 *television receivers in U.S. households during February–March, 1956. There were* 35,495,000 *homes with TV and* 1,694,000 *of them had more than one set. These figures mean that three out of every four U.S. households had TV sets at the time of the survey. In June 1955, only two out of three households had TV. The increase of sets within a time period of less than a year is more than* 3,000,000.

And, as we have taken to heart our Lord's missionary commandment, we seek also to use publicity and mass media in bringing His Gospel to men, women and children who are in desperate need of it. What we must carefully examine is, simply, whether the *means* can be correlated with the *end* that is sought. Even here, we cannot generalize. We must determine *which* means can be correlated with the end that is sought, and *which* cannot be correlated with it.

Bigness. That, too, we take for granted in our age and our society. Yet it is quite possible that we need increasingly to analyze, as Christians, such often ambiguous and decidedly relative terms as "bigness" and, to name another, "sincerity." At Evanston, it was said that "evangelism will be again the life-blood of the Church only when . . . laymen and laywomen all over the world begin to 'gossip the Gospel.' "[13] Canon Wedel has spoken of the need for a sharp increase in the number of "Christian dinner parties."

Dr. Graham mentions "modern techniques." I should say that, obviously, such techniques are to be claimed for Christ. He is their Lord as He is our Lord. Whether *claiming* certain techniques for Christ means *employing* them for Him, I am not certain. I use "claim" in this context in the most profound sense of our stewardship functioning under His sovereignty. For our stewardship to be at cross-purposes with His sovereignty would reduce our efforts to the level of the demonic. We must be as concerned with motivation as we are with new (or old) techniques, for motivation is being increasingly studied by the industry.

Ideas are pretested today by experts, so that public relations need not involve the wide element of gamble that once marked it. A personality can today be test-tube conceived and nourished on formula-idea pills and safe-attitude shots. The methods of publicity, bigness and modern techniques are being scrutinized carefully by the hucksters themselves, who use them all the time. The motivation underlying the methods is being discussed introspectively, not only along Madison Avenue and in Scarsdale, Beverly Hills and Greenwich, but in best-selling American fiction and nonfiction.

A. C. Spectorsky's *The Exurbanites* is written about those persons of tremendous influence in moulding public opinion who have moved out of the big city and beyond the suburbs to the "exurbs."

On every hand the results are visible, tangible, often depressing, and frequently comic; manners and morals, fads and foibles, furnishings and food; styles in clothes or in housing, in games or in sex . . . even in the pets the ideal U. S. family should take under its roof . . . all these are determined in Exurbia.[14]

Hollywood has made a film version of Al Morgan's novel, *The*

Great Man, which concerns the TV-radio business. In a key speech, a character named Ed Harris says:

When you get to be the Great Man, nobody has any real respect for you as a person. Nobody you work with, I mean. You're just a meal ticket to them if they're under your thumb. Or you're just a financial sheet to them if they're big brass. But they don't give a hoot in hell for you as a person. It would never occur to them to question any decision you make or are forced to make, to stop and say, does this violate this guy's integrity? [15]

What are the results of exploitation?

Much of mass communication within an entertainment category is powerfully moulding our thoughts and actions more than any overtly "educational" media. Herein one sees the gradual development of a new kind of tyranny (were the "bread and circus" days of Rome a tyranny?) This is a tyranny that is paradoxical and cannot effectively be labeled merely as tyranny; a tyranny that does not deprive us of necessities (unless a time to be quiet, to reflect, to analyze, is a necessity) but instead gluts us with luxuries; a tyranny that presents us incessantly with the clown on stage who so distracts our minds that we fail to think of where else we should be, and of what else we should be doing, on this clear afternoon.

Reinhold Niebuhr rightly points out that a civilization as technically efficient as ours "sets no limits to the standards which technics may achieve in establishing the security and comfort of the self against the hazards of nature or of history." [16] As a result, technical civilization has given the community a greater cohesion and intensity than any that prevailed in the agrarian societies; and, at the same time, technical civilization has emancipated the individual from his organic ties to the community. In this paradox exists an intensified tension between the individual and the community.[17]

The result is that there exists, by virtue of technological media, virtually a "captive audience" in a mass composed of many individuals who are islands, and psychologically isolated from one another, while physically being forced ever closer together. The average man or woman in large centers of population seems to be trying to make sense out of life in an age that is in many ways crushing him or her as a "person." He rides to work jammed into a bus or subway, or in a car that is jammed into a long line on a freeway or superhighway. His behavior patterns are moulded by forces pushing at him all the time. He works and plays with others in his particular peer-group, who keep him safely in line most of the time. He wants less to get ahead than to get along . . . or, simply, to belong. The "opinion leader" within each of various social strata has been identified by sociologists, who label as "horizontal opinion" leadership the fact that person-to-person communication seems to be taking place between persons on the same economic levels. Sociologist Paul Lazarsfeld speaks of personal influence as a kind of *detour of influence* from the mass media; the mass media information is detoured through an opinion leader to other persons. This is labeled "two-step communication." Ideas, it is found, travel along somewhat narrow strata, and not so much from one stratum into the next. However, a mass media or other kind of influence felt by one stratum will, in time, be felt by another stratum. This is what is meant by a "total cultural context of influence." This is actually a *web of communications.* In the midst of such a strident other-directedness as we find in our mass culture, it is tragically ironical that, as Mr. Eliot has forcefully put it, the desert is in the heart of our brother. David Riesman might have said that the desert is in the heart of one's peer-group.

William Ernest Hocking seems almost to suggest a form of needed therapy when he writes:

Through an untrammeled utterance meeting an equally untrammeled response, including such anger or contempt as the utterance may arouse, men discover their own wills and tastes, find confirmation or rebuke, mould their own growth and that of others. Expression is an experimental prelude of action: it is the explorative mid-world between thought and the commitment of deed; it is a growth function for all mental creation. There is, I believe, a common duty to protect the whole range of this freedom, as a right of social existence.[18]

This very *expression* is becoming lost. I believe that "the whole range of this freedom," mentioned by Professor Hocking, is in bitter jeopardy. The point is a controversial one. The press lord, the big advertiser in a medium, the man who controls tightly a good deal of the programming of a major TV network, the czar of a film studio and the banker whom he must appease and convince: all these persons maintain that, when the chips are down, they are really operating in the public interest, convenience and necessity. They argue vehemently that to impose a higher cultural level or educative level upon "the mass mind" than "the mass mind" desires would be sheer tyranny.

They argue that "message films" are wrong; yet all films are surely "message films," all films (as, indeed, all media of mass communication) vitally shake our attitudes or encase them in cement. The prime *raison d'etre* of many a newspaper has become entertainment, while an honest passion for truth has been forgotten. This is by no means true only of newspapers in America or any other single nation. The gutter press of Athens or Paris or London is as sensation-motivated, as entertainment-laden, as any paper America produces. Yet it must be pointed out that the contrast is particularly glaring between this latter-day entertainment concept in the United States and the reasons for this country's freedom of the press guaranteed by the Constitution. Under the cheap talk of "public interest," there is considerable exploitation of public interest in order to sell more newspapers. Too, as Professor Hocking has pointed out in his study, the pressure group power in the United States has reached staggering proportions, and this power is solidly felt in all media. Of course, it must be recognized that a combination of "public interest" and promotional opportunism on the part of a newspaper often results in an important exposé of corruption or revelation of concealed legitimate news in terms of a community's (and, indeed, the nation's) long-range state of health. An entertainment-oriented newspaper or magazine may well be the effective vehicle of such public service. This assumes vast significance when it means that a broad cross-section of the public is thereby presented with the first look at "news" prior to the study, by an elite within that broad cross-section, of a "trend" pointing the way to such "news." The role of "opinion leaders" is thus modified but perhaps not lessened.

Exploitation may take place for a "cause": to elect somebody to a political office, to erect a building (even a church building), to put through some kind of system that will ("it really will, eventually") make people better off and happier and better fed and better clothed. Yet isn't war, as we know it, the accumulation of many, many kinds of "sincere" exploitation? Collective sin as evidenced in a war is made up of many sins, such as pride, envy and hate, and of basic sin, which is always alienation from God. One of the worst forms of sin in exploitation is that form of pride which says: "I will exploit you for your own good." What, exactly, *is* this? Who can be objective enough to know what is this absolute kind of "good"? This can be influencing other persons to buy the most modern car, to eat the most scientifically produced breakfast food, to use the most foolproof new tooth powder, to elect the most foolproof politician, to adopt the most foolproof religion in order to be happy and rid of tensions in this life and to worship the most foolproof God.

Exploitation has become a norm in secular use of mass media. The possibilities of television, for example, are seen as follows, in an advertising "blueprint for television exploitation": the combination of sight-in-motion plus sound; a message can penetrate deeper and cling longer to the memory; the sales story can be controlled, step by step, to its conclusion; a product can be demonstrated quickly, effectively, to mass audiences; TV is face to face, person to person, and penetrates the family group itself. Already, though, it has been found by advertising experts that the television viewer is setting up defensive barriers to the commercialized battering ram acting on his intellect and emotions. It has been found, in research, that television is making the consumer wiser than radio did. The cruder attacks of advertising no longer have the telling effect they once did: the personal defensive barrier of sophistication toughens with the increase of knowledge. What to do? Psychological and sociological "depth" research is opening the field beyond the television viewer's "superficial barriers." Experts have already pinpointed "Mrs. Middle Majority," the composite housewife who represents the so-called American mass market.

An expert in motivation research in the advertising field explained in a talk before the Grocery Manufacturers of America how a food called kippers was being rejected at store counters by the American housewife:

So we found it necessary to examine the emotional associations people had with kippers. We found that kippers have a very foreign sound to most people. They visualize poor people in foreign countries who can't afford anything better, and minority groups in their own country. They think of dirty docks and foreigners with smelly boats. Most of their associations with kippers are both strange and unappetizing. What we found is that kippers are in a sense an un-American food. It's not what the good, middle-class housewife can safely serve to her friends. The advertising problem, therefore, was not to prove that kippers taste delicious. The problem was to Americanize kippers, to tie it in with accepted American foods, to make it familiar, to show how to use it, to show it against average, middle-class backgrounds in ordinary situations . . . to make it a perfectly safe, average, secure thing to serve.[19]

The primer accepted in today's advertising blueprint is that the consumer is basically selfish. This assumption is theologically sound. Accepted, too, is the fact that this selfishness must be exploited, developed, guided to the point of purchase. The advertiser in a mass medium of communication today carefully studies man's basic selfish motivations: self-preservation, ambition, love and economy. However, self-preservation has now been refined into this question: Can you protect me from the problems and worries of life? Ambition not only seeks to be a little better than the next-door neighbor; it now asks, rather tragically: Can you make me *belong?* Love is sex. Economy must appeal not only to the pocketbook but to pride: I like to think I'm shrewd, not a penny-pincher.

Goods have to be moved off of the store shelves. Competition is competition. Whatever attracts and builds audiences is featured on TV screens and radio shows, and in most newspapers. One cannot worry about trying to improve public taste when one must instead earn a living for his family by pandering to public taste. It is frequently noted, but generally only with a sigh, that the welfare of one's own children is inextricably tied up with "public taste," with the climate in which children are raised within society. An active Christian layman was confronted by a difficult dilemma not long ago. He was the program director for a television station. A fine program for children had not stood up competitively against the other children's programs running at the same viewing time on the other TV stations in his city. As program director, he had had to order the removal of the good children's program, and, at the insistence of the sponsor, to insert in its place a five-times-a-week horror-and-violence film series. Any other course of action would have cost him his job. He recognized the weight of the problem from the standpoint of Christian ethics; and he knew that his own children would be influenced by the "climate" he was helping to perpetuate.

One could fill many pages of statistics showing how a single medium of mass communication, television, is being employed to exploit a single segment of the United States population, children. Crime and violence are dominating factors in approximately 40 per cent of all programs presented specifically for children in the United States on television.[20] Yet the American Medical Association reported that crime programs made 76 per cent of a group of test children more nervous and increased their fears five-fold.[21]

In Chicago, a television columnist, Jack Mabley of the *Daily News,* publicized the findings of a survey of children's programs. The survey commenced on Christmas morning and extended through New Year's Eve of 1953, covering a one-week period. Thirty monitors, headed by a P.T.A. official, surveyed every children's program presented by the four Chicago TV stations during that time. The tabulation revealed that there had been 295 violent crimes portrayed exclusively on children's programs. These included 93 murders, 78 shootings, 9 kidnappings, 9 robberies, 44 gun fights, 2 knifings, 33 sluggings, 2 whiplashings, 2 poisonings and 2 bombings. The number of shows for children totaled 134. Of these 48 were western crime films; another 33 were old movies of various types. A film televised at 12:30 on a Sunday afternoon in Chicago showed two prisoners giving a clear explanation of how to kill with one swipe of a knife. Children watching this program also saw a girl murdered by being run down by a truck. On a Saturday afternoon at 2:30, a film advertised as "For the Whole Family" comprised the following elements: two violent deaths, laboratory experimentation in bringing dead persons back to life, the body of a dead woman rising from a casket, a plan to make an army of dead who would conquer the world, a body found in a car trunk, experiments on a living man, and two drownings.[22] The following statement was made before a Congressional subcommittee:

Young America, to a degree never before experienced, has been saturated with graphically illustrated murder, brutality and sadism. How can a youngster see so many human beings killed each week without acquiring an indifference toward violent death? Do not these things add up to a state of mind which breeds an acceptance of crime? How many among juvenile delinquents today would have been dissuaded from acts of delinquency had the youngsters with whom they associate looked upon these acts with clear disapproval? An overwhelming majority of experts and millions of parents are alarmed by these programs.[23]

Hollywood is nevertheless today producing television crime programs for children at a rate approximately four times greater than in 1951, according to a report issued by the National Association for Better Radio and Television.

Those who are involved in the use of mass media must ask themselves searching questions. Both the communicator and the person responding to the communicator stand under divine judgment. In the context of mass media, there are questions that might be directed to each, calling for a personal answer: Am I taking part in an immoral action? If there is a demonic element here, am I applying labels, naming devils? What is my Christian vocation, as a communicator, or as a listener, a viewer, a reader?

There are questions to be answered by the communicator: Am I exploiting my neighbor by studying his needs and desires, and by stimulating these in terms of new tastes; then, of new needs and desires? What is the dignity of man? Am I exploiting my neighbor for his own good (what does that mean?), or to set myself ahead in terms of money, position and power?

There are questions to be answered by the viewer, the listener or the reader, responding to communication: Am I being exploited? If so, exactly what does that mean? Am I powerless to do anything about it? Do I belong to myself or to God? May I, as a Christian, permit myself to be exploited in this way? If not, what may I do about it?

Significantly, a symposium sponsored by the National Conference of Christians and Jews on the subject of propaganda raised doubts as to the use of the "huckster approach" in promoting brotherhood. "There is a contradiction in promoting democratic values through the huckster approach," according to Professor Marie Jahoda, chairman of the panel. "The very nature of our organization means we are no sellers of soap."[24] A summary of views expounded at the symposium (and drawing heavily upon views contained in a paper prepared by Dr. Daniel Katz, Department of Psychology, University of Michigan) explained:

Both as a strategy and a philosophy, there are two significant approaches to propaganda. One appeals to the emotions of man, the other relies upon his reason. The first involves the professional propagandist, the "huckster," and seeks powerful stimuli to bring immediate results. The second presumes that techniques are less important than understanding. Rather, this view involves the ideologist who is committed to the long-range reconstruction, as a result of the progressively cumulative experience in learning, of individuals. There are those who would pose such distinctions as those marking trickery versus the aim to "know thyself." In any case, the establishment of these strategies and philosophies as distinctive, and incompatible, is essential in arriving at policies and practices for influencing people.[25]

One member of the symposium commented: "The Madison Avenue boys would be busy catching flies with sugar, when we may not want to catch flies at all."

I think that we must explore quite frankly into the nature of the question: Are we showing love for our neighbor when we give him "bread and circuses?" Many persons today would certainly answer in the affirmative. Is it possible that we may give our neighbor so much sugar-coated bread, and so many wonderful circuses, that we may make him sick in body and mind? Why are we giving our neighbor bread and circuses? Because we love him?(And, if so, who told us to love him?) Or, is it because we want to get a purchase, a vote, a reaction, out of him? Will that be good for him?

God speaks to each man in the world. God calls each man in the sense of vocation. This call can be a very uncomfortable thing, a disquieting and even a nerve-wracking thing. When answered honestly by man, this call destroys man's pride. (P. T. Forsyth asked the question: How much self-respect do you think Paul had left in him when he went into Damascus?) Do we love our neighbor so much that we will lay on the good, sweet, sensuous things until he may even be lulled away from, and numbed to, this disquieting call of God, which requires a decision and will shatter his peaceful presuppositions? Is it possible that our neighbor, avoiding God, may forget completely his having been created in the very image of God, if we penetrate deeply enough with enchantment, and add volume and increase the size and the motion of the moving distraction?

Seeing as the root of evil in human society the misuse of the power given to men (indeed, given to men as being made in the image of God), V. A. Demant goes on to state:

The worst perversions of human society occur in our day when men have reached the greatest power over the material creation.[26]

For Christians the transcendence of God over the world process is the ground of their claim that increase of knowledge and interdependence of men and groups of mere historical changes, without complete spiritual reorientation, do but render the forces of disruption more acute and painful.[27]

Nicholas Berdyaev saw the contemporary process of "dehumanization" moving in two directions, toward naturalism and toward technicism.

Man is subject to cosmic forces or to technical civilization. It is not enough to say that he subjects himself: he is dissolved and disappears either in cosmic life or else in almighty technics; he takes upon himself the image, either of nature, or of the machine.[28]

Mass media are bringing us closer together, yet (as would be expected) we are experiencing difficulty in becoming close in closeness, together in togetherness. In human encounter two egotisms come together. Garcin cries out, in Sartre's *Huis Clos:* "Hell is . . . other people!" Gabriel Marcel affords a Christian answer in Rose's statement, in *Le Coeur des autres:* "There is only one suffering: to be alone." Mass media are being employed to treat members of the mass audience as "objects" and not as "persons" who are known in "relationship" or "meeting." Empathy is achieving a bastardized kind of "personal" communication for general purposes of exploitation. "Personal" communication does not necessarily issue in what we call "meeting" between two "persons." We must distinguish between a demonic distortion of "personal" communication and Christian "personal" communication. The latter is grounded in the faith that the two "persons" communicating are doing so in the mutual experience and power of God the Holy Spirit, as sons of God equal in His sight, and as having been redeemed by the saving action of Jesus Christ. For a newspaperman, a film executive, an advertising copywriter, a clergyman making use of a mass medium of communication as a personality, what is the purpose of "closeness"? And are the recipients of communication in the category of "thou" or "it"?

The basic sin of exploitation lies in treating persons as objects. The Church cannot do this in the name of Christ.

We do not seek, in claiming TV or the press for Christ, simply to "use" them for Him. We have corrupted "use" so that it often means "exploit"; often the mass media are "used" so that we may thereby exploit other persons.

Again: we do not seek to "exploit" the TV industry or the press for Christ. We seek to help TV to be TV, the press to be the press, in terms of the will of God for each. His will being always mysterious, we shall be enabled to know it only by faith. Only in this sense do we "claim" these media for Christ: because they are His, and He is their Lord (both institutionally and in terms of the individuals working for them) as He is ours.

Surely (and this is the point we have been groping toward) we seek an expression of what is essentially our deep involvement in, and relation to, TV and the press and the other mass media. Let us realize, then, when we consider TV: that fantastic little wooden box in the living room which flashes fascinating pictures and emits strange sounds; which transforms the perhaps drab room into a glittering theatre for a couple of hours; which is wonderfully linked to millions of other little wooden boxes, and to a maze of connected equipment, and to a producer's mind and to the labor of many technicians; *even and also in regard to this,* God has created and has a purpose, Jesus Christ died upon the Cross and God the Holy Spirit is the Sanctifier.

THE CHURCH'S DILEMMA: TO EXPLOIT OR NOT TO EXPLOIT

What is to be the stand of the Church in response to this timely and insistent challenge?

The Church is hard pressed to adopt these same approaches in its own use of television for evangelizing the nonchurched. In many ways, the Church already, especially on small-station programs, is using many questionably overdramatized and huckstering techniques simply by virtue of the position of the Church within the age, within society. The mass communicator, whether he be a movie mogul, a TV automobile pitchman, a churchman reaching millions via a mass medium or a political figure, is automatically involved in moulding thought and action patterns of men, women and children. He is one of David Riesman's "culture diffusionists" who diffuse the taste judgments of the peer-group they belong to, to the other peer-groups lower down on the taste gradient. He is, in Russell Lynes' terminology, a "taste-maker." His responsibility is a great one.

It seems that the Church must play a dual role, speaking out against studied and highly developed exploitation of the emotions and desires of human beings, and, also, abstaining itself from such exploitation. To speak out is no easy task. We must speak out to a society that it is deeply involved in an exploiting and a being exploited that seem wholly natural to it, and yet are fundamentally not Christian. We are called upon to speak out to our friends, both communicators and those responding to communicators, telling them that they are taking part in an immoral action. H. A. Hodges speaks to this point:

People must be told, for it is a central point of Christianity, that their present values are wrong, not merely those which they themselves recognize to be self-centered, but even those of which they are really proud, and that neither in this world nor in Christianity can these be realized at all. Christianity does not exist to satisfy them as they stand, but to correct them; abolishing some, reforming the conception of others, and bringing to life new desires and insights of duty which were not there before. We can say that the Christian life which results from this is a life preferable in quality to any other that man can live, a life of knowledge and freedom; but it is a new life and in some ways a strange one, too.[29]

Ultimately, if the Church should slickly, effectively, knowingly succumb to enchantment, and thrust aside the Cross in order to attain "success"—then the Church could not speak as the Church to the very men it would confront in the highways and market places of life. The huckster may become baptized in a den of thieves but he will surely not see the place as a church. The Church, in renewed penitence, must always recognize the frightening degree to which it is already secularized. The Church is involved in the difficult paradox of the necessity to make use of what is also being used against itself. The Church cannot rely upon its own "objective" judgment as to the degree of its secularization, but, even while undergoing an intensive process of secularization directed against itself, must turn to Jesus Christ its Lord in penitence, renewed faith and hope. Never forgetting the paradoxical character of its own human leadership, the Church is called in its hours of fear and of despair to trust in itself not at all, but only in Christ Jesus.

Indeed, does the Church witness in strength or in weakness? Is its strength in its own weakness, and, at the same time, in the strength of Christ Jesus? The American poet, Delmore Schwartz, speaks of "witness":

"And I will always stammer, since he spoke,"
One, who had been most eloquent said, stammering.[30]

Karl Barth has interpreted "witness" in a moving way:

A man may be of value to another man, not because he wishes to be important, not because he possesses some inner wealth of soul, not because of something he is, but because of what he is . . . not. His importance may consist in his poverty, in his hopes and fears, in his waiting and hurrying, in the direction of his whole being towards what lies beyond his horizon and beyond his power. The importance of an apostle is negative rather than positive. In him a void becomes visible. And for this reason he is something to others: he is able to share grace with them, to focus their attention, and to establish them in waiting and in adoration. The Spirit gives grace through him.[31]

As we know, it is not easy to think and to act as Christians. Pagan "success" motivates us, at the same time that the Cross remains forever antithetical to worldly success symbols. Secular "publicity" has, alarmingly, blurred the focus with which we look at the Cross. P. T. Forsyth wrote:

Christ arouses antagonism in the human heart and heroism does not. Everybody welcomes a hero. The minority welcome Christ. We do resent parting completely with ourselves. We do resent Christ.[32]

Does this speak, not only to the content of our evangelical message, but also to the technique that brings that content to the masses? Who said the Cross is an easy thing, the Gospel a simple thing, success (even of our program of evangelization) an obvious thing, in the Age of Publicity any more than in any other age? We in the Church, in addition to criticizing social wrongs, must attempt to understand when we are evangelizing for Jesus Christ, in His grace, and also—and this is a dangerously subtle thing—when we have succumbed to the demonic even at this level, and are zealously "exploiting" persons for God in Christ, making "point of contact" with the sword or psychological depth research, or by selling Christ like soap. In this connection, Karl Barth speaks to us movingly and in a prophetic way. Surely, at present we are not sufficiently keeping the Cross in focus and withstanding the powerful lure of the success symbols of our age and our society. If a wrong implement or technique will place us, or keep us (and our message, our "position"), "at the top," have we the Christian humility, fortitude and strength to decline the exalted goal if it is not compatible with the required means? Publicity itself, and bigness and modern techniques, may create a decidedly non-Christian climate especially when publicity has become a substitute for merit.

Somehow, to violate the integrity of a person by exploiting him for Jesus Christ seems even more critical than exploiting him for a product, say Chrysler or Arrid or Paramount. One is not to condone the exploitation of man for any cause. Yet is not one actually blaspheming if he exploits the integrity of a fellow child of God and member of the human race, in what he assumes to be the interests of the Holy and Almighty God Himself? God never exploits man; He has created us with free wills. Jesus Christ, far from exploiting the situation in which He found Himself, refused all the temptations of worldly power; refused a crown; refused to press an "advantage," went off by Himself from the crowds and, actually, removed the element of passion that was present in the crowds; died alone, humiliated, defeated, upon the Cross. This is not only the antithesis but the refutation of exploitation. Indeed, love is always the antithesis and refutation of exploitation.

It should be said and said again: Let us not blame our own sins of exploitation upon the mass media or any other modern techniques or implements! These are, after all, machines and techniques of our making and operation. They dominate us only if we dominate one another by use of them, whether that use is intentional or merely "sincere." Such implements or techniques are as potentially good as they are evil. By all means, let us avoid the rotten theology and sinful pride of making modern techniques our own scapegoats. Let us avoid, too, the intellectual arrogance and sophisticated fantasy of looking down upon "popularization" and reaching out to people with the Good News of Jesus Christ in simplicity, lucidity and love. "Popular communication" is good. If we intellectualize the Gospel out of a man's comprehension, perhaps our sin is greater than we can fathom.

Obviously, to decide how *this* modern technique is usable in our work as Christians and how *that* modern technique is not, is anything but to retreat from "popular communication." It is, however, to exercise (in the words of Brother George Every) "Christian discrimination." We must determine the criteria for use or nonuse of specific techniques or implements that are at our disposal in Christian evangelism. The following might be among these criteria.

Is "sincerity" enough? "Sincerity" is contemporaneously about the highest compliment one can be paid, and about the most important element the mass communicator is supposed to possess. Frederic Wakeman, in his novel *The Hucksters,* spoke of a man's wearing a "sincere tie." David Riesman notes how the consumer "tends to respond to the performer as he responds to his business associates and politicians: in terms of personality, not performance." [33] He quotes some typical audience reactions to popular personalities in the entertainment world.

"I like Dinah Shore because she's so sincere," or "that's a very sincere record," or, "You can just feel he [Frank Sinatra] is sincere."
Again, sincerity means performance in a style which is not aggressive or cynical, which may even be defenseless, as the question-answering or press-conference technique of some politicians appears to be. The performer puts himself at the mercy of both his audience and his emotions. [The basis of judging] has shifted from the content of the performance and its goodness or badness, aesthetically speaking, to the personality of the performer. He is judged for his attitude toward the audience, an attitude which is either sincere or insincere. The performer of the nineteenth century appears to have been judged rather by his relations to his craft, that is, his honesty and skill.[34]

What is to be the Church's (or the representative communicator-churchman's) position in the mass media field: "aggressive," "cynical," "defenseless," "sincere"? If "sincere," how does an institution or individual cultivate such a trade-mark? What role does organized public relations have to play? If the Church or churchman cannot be both "sincere" and right about a particular issue, which will the Church or churchman choose to be? Is it not more important to seek the truth humbly than to be "sincerely" deluded?

Are we using modern techniques and implements to escape from reality? The machine, the TV set, the motion picture projector, may shield us from repentance but they will not be able to bless us with forgiveness. Men used to come together to hear Holy Writ. Many able-bodied men, women and children today hear Holy Writ and see it being read—and, in a mysterious way, even participate in the proceedings by sitting at home and watching church services on TV. This may remove the sting of relatedness and give one the feeling that he has given God a full hour, without having had to put up with other people. Although I do not wish simply to identify this category with a specific illustration, which would not give a true picture of the group as a whole, yet I will speak of two persons, a man and wife, whom I know, and of their experience. This is an able-bodied couple (with two cars in the garage, and living near several churches) which religiously observes Sunday morning at 11 o'clock by turning on the television for a full hour's telecast of a church service. This couple has a prejudice against certain types of other persons. The couple visited some half-dozen churches, even traveling considerable distances, trying to find a pure racial strain, or at least all pure white faces, in the congregation. Finally, visiting a cathedral nearby, the husband and wife saw the choir coming up the center aisle. "There were Jews, niggers and wops in it," the couple said; and now they never visit a church any more, but instead watch the services of Christ's Church over television.

Are we leading or seeking to lead persons for the wrong reasons? For example, there has been a conspicuous contemporary emphasis upon *using* God. This might well be one danger of even suggesting that the Gospel be promoted as well as soap! Is it not then a temptation to cut God down to our own size (at least, to try) by exploiting Him as a miracle product that will solve all ills?

Are publicity, bigness and modern techniques often merely increasing the volume and scope of a particular evangelical emphasis and masking the urgent task of converting to Christ basic alienation within society? We received the warning of a real danger in a World Council of Churches pre-Evanston study: here we were warned that the employment of methods that assume the existence of a Christian community

as a reality to which the lapsed may be recalled or into which the converted may be brought seems to result most often in at best, a warming of the hearts of those already within the Church and, at worst, a further alienation of those groups outside the Church's life.[35]

There needs to be fresh creative thinking for the task of making the Gospel relevant and deeply meaningful in situations of basic alienation within society. The report, cited above, spoke also of there being "too little indication of imaginative and fresh approaches to the task of evangelism." Here, does one not need a slower pace than is identified generally with bigness, publicity and modern techniques? Specifically, does not the "small technique"—that is, work on the local level—have a mighty role to play in the vital area of experimenting with new means of bringing into the Christian body alienated persons, especially among intellectuals and workers?

Is the integrity and essential freedom of the individual person sufficiently maintained and protected in our own efforts toward communication? Are we leaving the individual mind, body and feelings sufficiently unfettered in our use of tested techniques devised to ensure results? Or are we relying on emotional pressure, appeals to eroticism or fear of insecurity? Are we endeavoring to communicate, across the barriers of motivation which have risen higher with the leveling of mere technical obstructions, to a "thou" rather than to a mere "it"; in other words, are we sufficiently regarding "the audience" as comprised of persons to be valued rather than of objects to be manipulated? In our mass communication, when literal individual contact is impossible, are we retaining the concept of *personal* communication?

Psychological depth research is one of several new techniques being used increasingly to complement the use of mass media. Motivation research may seek to discern what "image" a person has of a car, a church, a wife, a president, a product, a god. If a man has the desired "image," the image that the propagandist wants him to have, then mass media can simply proceed to sell. If a man has an "image" not similar to the desired "image," that which he has must be remade before a sale, or a transaction, or a conversion, is made. Of course, the object itself—be it a car, a church, a wife, a president, a product, a god—might be altered; but it is more likely that the salesman or propagandist or manipulator, from the standpoint of his own "relatively objective" position, will choose to alter another person's "image" of a particular thing, rather than to change the thing itself.

An analysis of motivation research in *Fortune* makes the observation:

> *And in the future, the findings of M. R. may be still more extensively used by big corporations to meet the challenges of the fast-changing and increasingly complex and competitive American market. In that case, M. R. would certainly sharpen up some ethical questions, among them the question whether any manufacturer should exploit, as buying motives, the deepest human frailties that can be dug out by psychoanalytic method.*[36]

Motivation research makes some use of the basic kind of market research that has long been used. It goes further, however, in revising such tools of the trade as questionnaires and intensive interviews to uncover responses which are given psychological interpretation. M. R. then adds the use of various psychological tools, such as depth interviews, sentence completion, word association, Thematic Apperception and such other projective tests, which bring to the surface suppressed or unconscious consumer ideas, motives and feelings. M. R. claims to deal in "qualitative research" and it is criticized by some for its alleged lack of "quantitative proofs" of statistical research. M. R.

looks for psychological and sociological reasons for consumer buying. In doing so, it insists upon burrowing beneath the surface of conscious replies to questionnaires and, in fact, regards such replies as often being rationalizations.

Perrin Stryker writes that "M. R., in short, rejects the old marketing concept of economic man and loudly proclaims the concept of psychological man." He raises "a far more serious question about M. R. that has scarcely been mentioned even by its severest critics."

It is this: will the use of such a technique reinforce consumer motives and attitudes that advertisers might better leave alone? Fears about non-conformity, anxiety over security, narcissism, reluctance to face up to some of the disagreeable but necessary chores of life, excessive emulation of the Joneses—these and other signs of immaturity M. R. has unquestionably revealed. M. R. is undoubtedly an invasion of the consumer's privacy, but the real trouble with M. R. is not that it exposes such weaknesses but that it often seems to recommend, openly or implicitly, that U. S. business nourish these weaknesses and pander to them.[37]

Without implying any kind of generalized condemnation of motivational research activity (which is still a subject of considerable mystery and ongoing debate within the spheres of advertising, industrial relations and public relations), I should simply like to ask: Have we discerned sufficiently well the *depth of the possibilities* of such a new technique? Have we explored such frankly new areas in this technologically changing and psychologically analytical world, from a theological standpoint? Must not our Christian preparation—or lack of preparation—for such techniques be the factors determining our use or nonuse of them in specific instances?

This book examines a number of pitfalls into which some of the mass media have fallen at times and into which others may fall, or, rather, into which persons have fallen or may fall in their use of mass media. To generalize about the mass media is alien to the intent of the author. Specific instances have been pointed out to illustrate specific points. Since the industry exists naturally in an atmosphere of publicity and morale-building kudos, it does not seem the function of this book to add just another pat on the industry's back, but rather to examine some specific aspects of the industry critically and clinically. A warm regard for, and an immense appreciation of the industry, and its manifold social and potential contributions, is presupposed throughout this work. Only within the framework of such a presupposition, as indeed within a family structure, may the hardest and most searching examination be pursued in a spirit of love and quite obvious mutual involvement.

I have spoken critically of various media. I should like to speak enthusiastically of as many others. There have been unforgettably great experiences of the mass media in all of our lives. There are TV shows that we shall not cease to appreciate with the passing of time: Edward R. Murrow's vastly varied contributions to the medium; the documentary film on India, narrated by Chester Bowles; the superb film on mental illness, *Out of Darkness;* the imaginative work of the great comedians, especially that of Jimmy Durante; those musical and special-events telecasts, and especially a select list of TV dramatic presentations, about which we might reminisce together at great length and about which there would be a surprising unanimity of agreement. Our appreciation of any number of great motion pictures is still manifested by our keen interest in such craftsmen as screen-writers and directors, our participation, however disguised, in the cult of the star system, and our faithful attendance at reissue showings. A partial list of screen classics must include *City Lights, Citizen Kane, Bicycle Thief, Paisan, Camille, Ninotchka, Hamlet, Wuthering Heights, The King and I, My Little Chickadee, The 39 Steps, Dead of Night, Gone With the Wind, Lust for Life, Modern Times, The Informer, The Last Chance, Brief Encounter;* but such a list must include many films and must cover the wide range between *Nothing Sacred* and *Torment.* What of the many great French, Italian and British (and also those Swedish, German and Japanese) films that have been experiences of immeasurable artistic significance in our lives? We are all, whether or not we clearly come out and say it, very much indebted to, and grateful for, specific contributions of TV, motion pictures, radio and the press in the moulding of our tastes and attitudes. This is presupposed in this critique about mass media. It is of the utmost importance that the presupposition be emphatically understood by the reader.

A sharp and, indeed, searching criticism of various specific faults of the mass media—or, rather, of our misuse of the mass media—is not to be construed as a mass condemnation of the media. Nor is it to be construed as an implied suggestion that we, as Christians, should turn our backs upon the media. The implicit and total message of this book cries out loudly against such an interpretation of a portion book assumes the basic goodness of the media, dealing with our mistaken and often demonic use of them. This book ...s for granted our essential deep involvement with the media as ...ifestations and integral parts of the total culture in which we exist. Our Christian commandment and task is, obviously, to accept the implications of our basic involvement with the media. To do this we must certainly be wise as serpents and innocent as doves. We must, in the sovereign power of God the Holy Spirit, fearlessly accept a basic, unselfrighteous and unpremeditated involvement with the persons and institutions and techniques of the mass media. At the same time, we must remember who we are. We are Christians, we belong to God and not to ourselves, we live in the perfect freedom of the lordship of Christ. So, our total involvement will be a Christian total involvement. We will be immersed in the world, yet not worldly. Our feet will be firmly planted on the earth, and we will never despise the earth that God created, yet our hearts will rest in the peace which passes all understanding, which is the peace of God in the risen Christ. This will be a peace in tension. "In the world ye shall have tribulation: but be of good cheer; I have overcome the world." We shall not forget to ask for Christian tension in the midst of unchristian peace, nor for the peace which passes all understanding in the midst of the Christian's war.

The problem facing us—that of use or nonuse, in specific times and places, of specific implements and techniques of our "modern" age—is a complex one of considerable depth. It touches in a paradoxical way upon our total involvement with such devices as the media of mass communication. We must ask ourselves hard questions. Is our task that of exploiting bodies and minds by sword and pen, guns and films, for this Lord who became weak and emptied Himself for our sakes; or is our task that of surrendering sword and pen, guns and films, to Him, and emptying ourselves so that He may work through our "emptiness"—which is, in fact, a necessary act of surrender before the triumph in us of His grace? When does evangelism become exploitation? Is the Church free to "exploit" for Jesus Christ and for the Kingdom of God? When is a technique (even a "religious" technique) *really* religious—indeed, Christian—and when is it not? The answers, arrived at amidst all the publicity and bigness of the climate in which we live, might well confront us with a cross roads in our mass evangelistic task.

We must repeat, the task is difficult; but we cannot afford to retreat from it. We must ask the theologian:

Do the mass media represent simply vulgarization, popularization, an area of mounting confusion with which you cannot cope? Is your theology not applicable to this major crisis in Christian life and communication? Have you nothing to say about the media which are, in fact, influencing and educating your own children, perhaps even more than their schools and churches? Translate your too-big words into words which the people of less education than you can understand, and speak to them. Help them to understand what is happening to them, to the world in which they (and you) live. What does God say about an alternative to 1984 and "big brother"; what ought the Church as the Church, *to be doing about mass media on their staggered levels of relevant concern to man?* [38]

And the "activist" Christian, who is producing "bigger and better" religious films, TV programs and publications, must be asked:

What is a religious medium of communication? What is Christian communication? What are your own motives? Obviously, they will not be "pure" motives, but what are they? And are they offered, in their sinful condition, to Christ?

Our evangelical task is clearly cut out for us. The work will require the theologian to dirty his hands in a disreputable new field for him, and will require the sincere activist to call a halt, shake hands with the theologian and, having picked up some unbelievably needed pointers, move on again, but more slowly. We all need a change of pace, and we can learn what our own pace needs to be only from each other, in the dynamic power of God the Holy Spirit.

FOOTNOTES FOR THE AGE OF PUBLICITY

1 Louis Kronenberger, *Company Manners,* p. 133.
2 "Madam Ambassador Clare Boothe Luce. Her Versatile and Crowded Years," *Newsweek,* p. 28, Jan., 24, 1955.
3 "The New Evangelist," *Time,* p. 38, Oct. 25, 1954.
4 The Church—"Christ's Holy Catholic Church, that is, the whole congregation of Christian people dispersed throughout the whole world." This definition, found in the 55th Canon of the Church of England, is presupposed throughout this work.
5 *Evanston Speaks* (Reports from the Second Assembly of the World Council of Churches), pp. 32–33.
6 Address to the seventeenth General Council of the World Presbyterian Alliance. Reported in the New York *Herald-Tribune,* Aug. 4, 1954.
7 Thomas Whiteside, "The Communicator," *The New Yorker,* p. 38, Oct. 16, 1954.
8 Soren Kierkegaard, *For Self-Examination,* pp. 71–72.

[9] John Hotchkiss, "The Battle for Men's Minds," *The New Statesman and Nation,* p. 380, Oct. 2, 1954.
[10] Alec Vidler, *The Theology of F. D. Maurice,* p. 8.
[11] "Profile—Billy Graham," *The Observer* (London), p. 3, April 24, 1955.
[12] "Billy Graham Answers His Critics," *Look,* p. 47, Feb. 7, 1956.
[13] *Evanston Speaks,* op. cit., pp. 28–29.
[14] A. C. Spectorsky, *The Exurbanites,* p. 8.
[15] Al Morgan, *The Great Man,* p. 288.
[16] Reinhold Niebuhr, *The Self and the Dramas of History,* p. 20.
[17] *Ibid.,* p. 36.
[18] William Ernest Hocking, *Freedom of the Press,* p. 97.
[19] Dr. Virginia Miles, "What Makes People Do Things?," address delivered before the Grocery Manufacturers of America at the Greenbriar, June 21, 1955.
[20] Richard Clendenen and Herbert W. Beaser, "The Shame of America," *The Saturday Evening Post,* p. 85, Jan. 22, 1955.
[21] Los Angeles *Herald-Express,* p. 1, Sept. 5, 1952.
[22] "Jack Mabley Launches Anti-Crime Crusade," *TV Magazine,* Jan., 1953.
[23] Clendenen and Beaser, *op. cit.,* p. 85.
[24] "Christians, Jews Group Says It Believes in Advertising; Symposium Views Not Its Own," *Advertising Age,* pp. 2, 6, Nov. 21, 1955.
[25] *Ibid.*
[26] V. A. Demant, *Christian Polity,* p. 24.
[27] *Ibid.,* p. 26.
[28] Nicholas Berdyaev, *The Fate of Man in the Modern World,* p. 25.
[29] H. A. Hodges, *Christianity and the Modern World View,* p. 75.
[30] Delmore Schwartz, "The Starlight's Intuition Pierced the Twelve," *The Kenyon Review,* pp. 383–85, Summer, 1944.
[31] Karl Barth, *The Epistle to the Romans,* p. 33.
[32] P. T. Forsyth, *The Work of Christ,* pp. 21–22.
[33] David Riesman, *The Lonely Crowd,* p. 158.
[34] *Ibid.,* p. 220.
[35] *Evangelism—The Mission of the Church to Those Outside Her Life,* (An Ecumenical Survey prepared under the auspices of the World Council of Churches), p. 25.
[36] Perrin Stryker, "Motivation Research," *Fortune,* p. 146, June, 1956.
[37] *Ibid.,* p. 232.
[38] This and the following quotation is from Malcolm Boyd, "The Crisis of the Mass Media," *Christianity and Crisis,* pp. 70–72, May 28, 1956.

RELIGIOUS COMMUNICATION BY THE MASS MEDIA

INTRODUCTION It is essential that we realize we are all being conditioned, educated, influenced and acted upon, continuously, by the media of mass communication. All media are "message" media, moulding our thought and action patterns—particularly when we are unaware of the ongoing process.

Generally, we are unaware of the impact of the mass media. There are times, however, when we brace ourselves for the impact. These are when we *know* we are about to become the recipients of somebody else's ideas. This suspicion may assert itself as the clergyman makes his way into the pulpit and prepares to commence his sermon; when the curtain is about to go up on a "message" play, labeled as such by a critic or by a foolish press agent; when we see, on TV, a political candidate, a noted philosopher or a religious leader. Suspicion whispers that at this point one should slip unobtrusively out of the church pew, storm out of the theatre or snap off the TV set. The recipient of a message considers that he is about to become a guinea pig.

The persons and ideas that we do take seriously, we regard not only with suspicion, but often with resentment: they are trying to *influence* us! It is ironical that:

> *Unfortunately nothing affects us so much as that which we do not take seriously. "The unacknowledged legislators of the world" are not the serious poets, whose doctrines are approved or dissolved upon critical examination, but popular writers . . . and the makers of film scenarios.*[1]

What happens when we are aware that we are going to receive the impact of onrushing ideas, and we have braced ourselves for the slap? All of our preconceptions in regard to the person who is imparting the ideas come to the fore. This is true whether the person is a political candidate, a Communist, a clergyman, a scientist or a Hollywood star. This presents an unusual and great problem for the person who is openly and manifestly imparting ideas. A lack of frankness is somewhat unrealistic in an age when everyone is fairly bristling to determine "the line" or "the point" of everyone else.

All media of mass communication are theologically relevant and important. Today the more influential creative work is being carried on by persons who instruct us without, generally, being aware that they are doing so. The person who is suspicious of the clergyman's intentions waits without suspicion for the message of Ava Gardner, Jackie Gleason, Frank Sinatra and Marilyn Monroe. What's their line? Entertainment. Let's relax and enjoy it. Sure, go ahead; but don't forget that entertainment, like big business, like communism or any other rival religion, has a gospel and sacraments and its own "salvation."

EXPLICIT CHRISTIAN COMMUNICATION

It is essential that we plan our evangelistic efforts, from a mass media standpoint, in two parallel ways. We surely must continue to develop the explicitly "religious" channels of mass communication. Also, we must strive to interpret in understandable Christian theological terms for the layman the vast majority of mass media offerings that are consciously trying only to entertain—but that are, in fact, decisively moulding the thought and action patterns of men and women within our society.

A significant report from the Evanston Assembly of the World Council of Churches notices the role played by mass media in modern life and advocates Church use of such implements. The document reads, in part:

We face today the overwhelming impact of the cinema, radio and television, as well as the greater perfection of posters, newspapers, and magazines. The result is that the convictions and decisions of individuals in many countries are reached under the pressure of a common mental climate which these media of mass communication tend to create. Hence the Christian Church must use these same media; for it is essential that Christianity, the questions it asks and the answers it offers, should permeate the general consciousness, if the ground is to be prepared for individual decision for Jesus Christ.[2]

We have too often overlooked the importance of all art forms as means of communication. The statement was made about Simone Weil that she approached her encounter with God through two art forms acceptable to the most anti-Christian: Gregorian chant and metaphysical poetry.[3] Art forms may be channels of God's grace, instruments of communicating man's understanding of God's pursuing will and love, as well as man's response.

Miss Dorothy L. Sayers has provided us with a highly laudable statement of purpose and technique regarding the preparation of a series of "religious" programs for radio broadcasting. She wrote:

My object was to tell that story to the best of my ability, within the medium at my disposal . . . in short, to make as good a work of art as I could. For a work of art that is not good and true in art is not good or true in any other respect, and is useless for any purpose whatsoever . . . even for edification . . . because it is a lie, and the devil is the father of such. As drama, these plays stand or fall. The idea that religious plays are not to be judged by the proper standard of drama derives from a narrow and lop-sided theology which will not allow that all truth . . . including the artist's truth . . . is in Christ, but persists in excluding the Lord of Truth from His own dominions.[4]

One might say that Miss Sayers is restating a self-evident truth. Unfortunately, if it is such, it is not self-evident to a number of persons engaged in "religious" mass media efforts.

There is a startling lack of fresh, creative approaches in efforts made in this field. This becomes the more startling when one realizes the intense creative aspects of the Christian life. The sparsity of fresh, creative thinking along lines of Christian use of mass media is ironical when one recalls how the Church is interested in a soul among souls, in one man in a crowd of men, an individual located in the midst of a computed mass of persons. However, more frequently than not, the Church has failed to reach the individual in the crowd when it has used mass communications media. The Church has been completely unable to stop the process of secularization, Dr. W. A. Visser 't Hooft said in a lecture at the Chateau de Bossey. Then, he made the telling point: The Church has been on the defensive, rather than creative.

Why has the Church not been creative?

A number of answers to this question would be advanced by various persons. One of these would surely concern the Church's fundamental understanding of itself as the Church, its understanding of its mission and of all evangelism. It is apparent that the Church must undergo a continuing process of renewal, if it is to move freshly from honest self-examination toward communicating to the world the nature of its essential mission. Its ongoing mission, in fact, waits upon honest self-examination, penitence and renewal within the dynamic power of God the Holy Spirit. The ongoing mission will remain the groundwork of all Christian communication.

Specifically, at the mass media level, we must consider a factor that breeds confusion and distorts creative efforts. What is the audience for a "religious" medium of mass communication? The New Haven study of religious broadcasting and telecasting has shown how important it is to distinguish "minority audience" from "majority non-audience." This indicates the possibility that a large number of clergy and others involved in "religious" mass media might be in a confusing muddle marked by a discrepancy between ends and means. They might be trying to reach outside the fold of the Christian faithful with the Gospel message, while, at the same time, by the nature of their presentation, be sharply limiting their audience to members of the faithful core. The study within New Haven produced this comment:

In research on broadcasters' conception of the "Target Audience," the conclusion is evident that most religious programs are conceived of as means whereby a religious in-group can make some contact with the multitude outside the fold. Actually, the audience is composed almost wholly of the faithful rather than of potential converts . . . One is forced to the decision that few of the broadcasters have any clear picture of the audiences which their programs actually reach.[5]

The sponsors of religious programs generally state their aims and identify their "target audiences" in broad and sweeping terms, indicating in most cases a failure to focus on specific groups or to delineate specific purposes to be achieved by these programs.[6]

The former Director of Religious Broadcasting for the British Broadcasting Corporation firmly stated that the *primary objective* of religious broadcasting "is to communicate the Christian Gospel to listeners with whom the Churches have few other effective means of contact."[7] This must remain the primary objective of all religious broadcasting and of religious telecasting. It is an objective seldom successfully realized in practice. When one hears a number of religious radio programs, or watches various religious telecasts, it is apparent that very often the producers are either overlooking the objective stated above, or else are floundering in an attempt to realize it. They seem to be missing the mark because they do not understand their audience. If a producer (as has actually happened) reacts strongly against treacly organ music, an unctious announcing quality, deadeningly monotonous script material and mediocre, blunted techniques found in some religious broadcasting and telecasting, he will not really improve matters if he is motivated too strongly by mere "reaction." This frequently manifests itself in "shocking" tactics which alarm the faithful and befuddle those outside the fold, who are not thereby attracted to the Church at all. The Christian faith is simply made to look ridiculous by many such extremists who "react" too violently against an extremist conservatism. Often, in either extreme position, the Gospel itself seems to be forgotten (certainly, it is not proclaimed), and technique becomes the end desired and exalted.

Many an important radio and television sponsor, before launching a new program, uses not a "huckster" but a sound research approach in determining exactly what audience is desired and available. It is determined whether network radio or TV will do the sales job best, or whether the sales message should be "pinpointed" in individual markets. It is asked: Is the sales message being geared to persons who do not know the product or company name; or to persons who are familiar with the name and are buying a company product, and are now asked to buy a new product made by the company; or to persons who are asked to continue buying the same product as before? In the case of a religious broadcast or telecast, such a question as this one might well be asked: Are we trying, *with this particular program,* to reach the churched or the unchurched? Waiting upon the answer might well be such factors as terminology, imagery, the physical background, indeed the whole method of approach. Danger lies ahead when the answer is not sought. Old prejudices may simply be aroused; misinformation may be dealt with quite unintelligently; a producer may fail to face up to his audience as it *is,* in contrast with what he might wish it to be.

"Up-to-date techniques" is a loaded term. Obviously, it should not become an end in itself. Inversely, a summary rejection of the term cannot be excused. Many techniques that are very poor, some of which are "shocking" and without any other intrinsic meaning, are mistakenly called "up-to-date." We have reached out via mass media to such segments of our audience as "the teen-ager" or "the housewife" or "the businessman" or "the aged" with various gimmicks, which we have often labeled as "up-to-date techniques." Most of the gimmicks have been pretty old stuff. Also pretty old is the assumption that a particular group of people will be reached by a program geared to the taste of the mass audience of which the group is a segment.

We can learn from the example of the B.B.C. Third Programme in England, which can be planned for a particular listening audience, as the segment of the total available radio audience listening to the Third Programme is rather clearly delineated. An example of some fresh, creative thinking on the Third Programme was a series recreating famous Christian sermons by such preachers as John Donne, Charles Kingsley, Lancelot Andrewes, Bernard of Clairvaux and John Wesley, to cite a few. A particularly dramatic re-creation of a sermon was that dealing with St. Bernard's preaching the twenty-sixth in his famous Sermons on the Canticles, in which St. Bernard abruptly departed from his theme (a commentary on the first two chapters of the Canticles, or Song of Songs) to give a panegyric on his deceased brother, Gerard. The same series re-created several New

Testament sermons, including St. Paul's speech to Agrippa (a free translation of Acts 26 by the Rev. J. B. Phillips), the Sermon on Mars Hill and St. Peter's Sermon on the Day of Pentecost.

Religious broadcasting and telecasting has to achieve its impact upon an audience without being obvious about achieving that impact. A leading trade journal review of two individual programs in a religious TV series is of interest because it points up this problem:

A virtue of both programs, and presumably of the whole series, is that there is no involved pitch for the church or any arm thereof. At the beginning it says merely that this is the Catholic Hour. *The story begins and continues straight through without interruption. At the close there is notice of the sponsor, and an address if the viewer wants further information. The viewer gets an entertaining drama, an idea he can accept or dismiss, and no haranguing.*[8]

Both from a standpoint of basic motivation and of technique growing out of it, there needs to be stronger local integration of nationally produced radio and TV programs. The "technique" is not only at the heart of the motivation underlying such production, but also infinitely increases the impact in individual circumstances that can be guided.

When speaking of impact, we must consider the tragic absence, from the vast majority of mass media efforts that are labeled "religious," of the scandal of the Gospel. We generally observe a comfortable, lukewarm version of the Gospel, which is said to fit in with "public welfare" on an ethical basis quite cozily, and qualifies for free time in the eyes of the FCC. "A little religion is a good thing for everybody." This fails, however, to disturb anyone with the challenging Person of Jesus Christ. In his now famous New York speech in which he discussed religious broadcasting, Dean Liston Pope of Yale University criticized "many so-called religious programs" as being "neither intelligible nor intelligent from a Christian point of view."[9] Conceivably, in addition to workshops conducted by professional TV and radio personnel for churchmen, there need to be more workshops conducted for the professional personnel by churchmen. This would in no way solve, however, the lack of preaching the scandal of the Gospel by churchmen themselves. Again, in this instance, only Church renewal will awaken churchmen to the full scope and dimensions of the Gospel content. Professional public relations and mass media men and women need to understand the motivation of Christians in seeking mass media facilities, time and space, "to magnify the Lord." Before this, however, Christians must themselves be renewed in their convictions and mission "to magnify the Lord."

Too many Christians believe that a good motive compensates for a weak, poorly constructed and produced program or film or publication. We must not forget that a church is competing for audience attention in an increasingly competitive area of available time and space. We cannot overlook, either, the many types of entertainment competing for the average person's available hours in each day. In television, on a network basis in the United States, the possibility of a church's presenting a program without audience appeal has become virtually nonexistent. The industry's lifeblood is good programs that will attract audiences and sponsors. A good rating structure deteriorates in the case of a weak link. The answer to badly written, directed and produced programs, films or publications is good craftsmanship and sound creative work grounded in professional experience. This costs money.

Consequently, the idea of sustaining, noncommercial religious programs (and low-budgeted, severely limited film productions and publications aimed at mass audiences) must be reappraised. If a radio or TV program, for example, is to compete with other programs (in such respects as creative ingenuity, acceptable craftsmanship, creditable treatment in promotion and time placement) commercial sponsorship is generally needed. Either an individual church must put up the money (as in the case of the Lutheran-produced dramatic series, *This Is The Life*) or else commercial sponsorship must be acceptable, and therefore desirable, to both commercial sponsor and church. The Bishop Sheen series is an example of the latter. Important issues are raised by the question of commercial sponsorship of a religious program. Is there too close an identification between church and sponsor? Does a church appear to have a price tag, if it accepts commercial sponsorship? Can a church speak out against the moral abuses inherent in hucksterized mass media if it is on a sponsor's pay roll?

The wording of the above questions is crude. To be a bit subtler, let us ask: Is there an essential difference between accepting commerical sponsorship of a particular church TV program and, on the other hand, accepting an advertisement from the same sponsor for inclusion in a church magazine or newspaper?

To permit the problem to reach a deeper level, let us consider the question of a church layman who is employed by a company that is not acceptable as the sponsor of a church telecast. Perhaps this layman works in the advertising or promotion department of the company. What has the church in question to say about this layman's secular occupation? Is he "sinning" by continuing in his job?

These questions, if honestly considered, become quite complicated. We must remember the dual nature of the Church. It is, first, the Body of Christ, the Bride of Christ, the extension of the Incarnation. It is, secondly, a social-historical institution, filled with sinners in various stages of honest repentance, and caught up in the same social and economic sins marking the culture of which it is an identifiable part. The first nature of the Church stands in judgment, not only upon the other institutions that exist alongside the Church within a culture, but upon the second nature of the Church also. The Church in its social-historical institutional sense may stand convicted, by the Church as the Body of Christ, of a sinful, prideful self-righteousness. Therefore, the Church cannot simply arbitrarily dismiss "commercial sponsorship" of one of its programs as "unfitting." It is, in its second nature, a part of its culture, along with the company that may sponsor one of its "religious" programs. The Church, as a social-historical institution, may not hand down a blanket condemnation of free enterprise while dependent upon free enterprise for its own economic survival, or of commercial enterprises (with all their moral ambiguities) while engaged itself in the employment of fund-raising organizations and of full-scale promotional activities.

There have been desperately few honestly effective Church radio or TV presentations, if we are bearing in mind Gospel content and techniques that do not contradict the content they should convey. "Religious" broadcasting-telecasting history in the United States is marked by the use of a few outstanding personalities. The more conspicuous among these have been Fosdick, Sheen, Sockman, Peale and Graham. Oral Roberts is in another category. The TV success of a Fulton J. Sheen actually obscures a vital point. His success is that of a dynamic, intelligent personality, ideally suited to the video medium. It does not come from a triumphant wedding of Church and industry in terms of production, writing, direction or creative approaches that are refreshingly new.

A clergyman making such full use of mass media becomes a celebrity. In the steel mills of Sheffield, England, I was asked most frequently to discuss two American personalities, Miss Marilyn Monroe and Dr. Billy Graham. This is not surprising, when one bears in mind the tremendous mass media promotional efforts behind these two personalities: films, TV, radio, magazines in all countries, newspapers, references in books, posters and signboards. The Church needs to be warned not to use an excessively "superballyhoo" approach as a means of proclaiming the Word and Sacraments of God in Christ. An example of excessive "superballyhoo" can be found in an overidentification of the Church with big-name personalities, as a kind of personality panacea for the whole project of attracting people to Christianity. A strange temptation confronting us is the fact that "the stars in the celluloid heaven are as real to twentieth-century man as were the saints to man in the Middle Ages."[10] An even stranger phenomenon is the fact that many churchmen are themselves becoming celebrities by virtue of mass media, and are remaining "on top" by virtue of their continued use of mass media. This throws into bold relief, in another way, the question of the Church's deep involvement in mass media, commercial competition and high-pressure salesmanship. The mass media reach out to make new celebrities. A *Time* cover story, a *Life* layout, a TV film documentary, of a retiring, introspective theologian, for example, immediately makes him a celebrity, too; and he is instantly caught up in the very process that he may be at work criticizing as a "paradox" in his latest tome being written within ivy-covered seminary walls.

In the field of religious publications, a trend is seen towards innovations in Christian journalism on a popular, mass scale. *Church Illustrated,* in England, represents an attempt to publish a Christian magazine of general public interest. *The Open Door,* in Holland, is designed to appeal to people who are accustomed to reading general illustrated magazines, and it tries to speak "to ordinary people in everyday language."

Religion is prominently represented on the lists of best-selling books in both fiction and nonfiction categories. Religious subjects are featured increasingly in the mass-selling magazines, and attracting readers. In the week that *Life* presented its "Christianity" issue, *Look*'s leading article was a piece by Justice Douglas on religion in Russia.

"MUSIC BUSINESS GETS RELIGION" was *Variety's* banner headline (Sept. 5, 1956). The paper documented the statement "Big

Disk Coin in Bible Belt" with mention of such popular records as "I Believe," by Jane Froman, "He" by Al Hibbler, and "Somebody Up There Likes Me," by Perry Como. There is also a big retail market, it is reported, for "sacred music, gospel artists, and the like."

Hollywood has periodically "discovered" the commercial possibilities of religion. This fact has offered us lately a record number of motion pictures which the trade paper, *Variety,* places in a category called "religioso." Religion has become "boffo boxoffice," and an unprecedented number of important films with religious themes are paying off. Religion, in becoming grist for the mill of the moviemakers, has been used as a lure for box-office dollars, as a period cloak for depicting profligate living, as a gold mine of story material with a universal kind of appeal, as a source of strength and inspiration and as a proclamation of the action of God in Christ. Seldom has a single motive stood alone; the strands of motivation have been overlapping and sometimes conflicting.

Early in this century there were numerous screen portrayals of the life of Jesus Christ. When the 1912 film, *From the Manger to the Cross,* was shown, exhibitors were advised by a public relations man that just a small amount of incense should be burned in the theatres a short time before the arrival of the audience. However, it was declared inadvisable that ushers should be garbed in surplices.[11] By 1926, a gaudier day had arrived in movie exploitation. A reviewer complained about the lavish M.G.M. production of *Ben Hur*:

> Ben Hur, *as General Lew Wallace imagined and wrote it, was a comparatively simple story of the Christ. When the novel was dramatized, it became essentially a spectacle; now, on the screen, it is about one million times more of one . . . and the resultant orgy of huge sets, seething mobs and camera effects contains little of the spirit of the original story.*[12]

A reviewer for a motion picture trade paper was overpowered by the film and wrote:

> *What matter the Chinese worship their idol or the barbarian the sun or the Gentiles Jesus or the Jews God? Those who worship, whether at altar or pew, worship to their faith. Faith is humanity and humanity is the brotherhood of man . . . that's Ben Hur.*
>
> *The church of any denomination or faith will get behind Ben Hur. It's bigger than the book a Christian wrote; it's bigger than the play a Jew produced; it's the bigger lesson to teach the world, wide and far, what*

faith is, and as here adapted, directed and film-produced by Christian and Jews, bigger than all of the writings, all of the teachings, and all of the missionaries. Ben Hur is the greatest single thing for religion, for the theatre, for the church, for the stage and screen, and for the masses, high and low, ever uttered.[13]

In 1916, Thomas Ince had made the film, *Civilization,* a strange, allegorical picture depicting Christ wandering in a place called "Borderland" which supposedly lay between earth and eternity. The same year saw the production of D. W. Griffith's colossal and controversial epic film, *Intolerance.* The conflict of Jesus with the Pharisees, with the Jewish rabbinate and with Rome was depicted.

In *Ben Hur,* Christ is never seen in close-up. We see in the distance, in the dense crowd packing the route to Calvary, the Christ-figure in a shining white, flowing robe, as he struggles along with the heavy, wooden cross. A study of this scene reveals that all the other persons in it are clothed in dark garments. Along the route we see three women of Jerusalem, garbed in black for mourning, kneel down and ask the Christ-figure (out of camera range) for a blessing. The screen reveals the hand of Christ, with the sleeve of a flowing white robe, held over their heads. In a night scene at Calvary, the camera shows the feet of the crucified, as Roman soldiers gamble beneath the crosses and a few mourners remain in the gathering darkness.

The 1927 production by Cecil B. DeMille of *King of Kings* has been seen, according to a 1953 "conservative estimate," by 900,000,000 people. It is still shown about 1200 times a year in the United States alone. A missionary in India, who replaces his old print every three years, has shown the picture to 125,000 persons. More than 600 prints of the film are in world-wide circulation. The picture's titles have been translated into 23 languages. Each Lenten season *King of Kings* committees of clergymen in principal cities throughout the world have sponsored its showing in local theatres.[14]

During the shooting of the film, H. B. Warner, who portrayed Christ, was ordered to spend his time on the motion-picture set in solitude. He ate his meals alone and wore a veil on his way to and from the dressing room. Mr. DeMille stated that he wanted Warner to be as reverent toward the role as was humanly possible. An advertisement printed in newspapers in 1926 reads: "The King of Kings is magnificent . . . dazzling . . . awesome . . . inspiring. . . . It is the most stupendous achievement of the cinema art . . . a picture with a thousand scenes of beauty and power. Eighteen stellar players, 5,000 persons in the ensembles. . . . It is a screen production enthusiastically acclaimed by press and public thru-out the world. History's Most Sublime Drama."

Hollywood in 1932 released a picture made by Mr. DeMille and entitled *Sign of the Cross.* Here is a review published in a trade paper at that time:

Religion triumphant over paganism. And the soul is stronger than the flesh. Religion gets the breaks, even though its followers all get killed in this picture. It's altogether a moral victory . . . Neat, deft, and probably beyond reproach is the manner in which the scarlet punches are inserted. Every sequence in which religion wins out is built upon lurid details. The censors may object to the method but they can't oppose the motive, and in the way Cross was produced one can't be in without the other.[15]

The story dealt with the merciless rule of Nero over the Christians. The emphasis on torture was strong and embellished with details: a small boy tortured on the rack, Amazon women impaling midgets on the ends of their spears, men breaking each others' backs, nude girls fed to alligators, elephants made to walk on chained prisoners.

In more recent times, Hollywood has given us *The Robe, David and Bathsheba, Samson and Delilah* and *Demetrius and the Gladiators.* Of *The Silver Chalice,* a recent Hollywood "religious" picture, a reviewer mentioned that it, like *The Robe,* had a *thing* as hero. He commented:

The thing in this picture is the cup which Jesus used at the Last Supper. Because he used it, the picture suggests, it has a kind of intrinsic power of its own. The cup excites religious veneration and awe when it is carried into the room; people fall down on their knees and choral music swells to a crescendo in the background. The Silver Chalice *does not go quite so far as* The Robe *and suggest that this power can even affect the unbeliever, but it comes perilously near this implication.*[16]

The ministry, almost always in terms of the Roman Catholic priesthood, has been a popular subject in such films as *Going My Way, The Bells of St. Mary, I Confess, The Fugitive, Edge of Doom, Boys Town, Fighting Father Dunne, Keys of the Kingdom, The Song of Bernadette, The Miracle of the Bells, On the Waterfront* and *The Left Hand of God.* Gilbert Seldes made this observation anent *The Bells of St. Mary:*

The jaunty priest of Bing Crosby, the athletic nun of Ingrid Bergman, created new images in the American mind, drastically altering old stereotypes; the Protestant minister and the rabbi were denied this freshening contact with the people.[17]

Gregory Peck, Frank Sinatra, Bing Crosby, Pat O'Brien, Barry Fitzgerald, Spencer Tracy, Charles Bickford, Dana Andrews, Montgomery Clift and Humphrey Bogart are among the top male stars who have portrayed Roman Catholic priests on the Hollywood screen. Richard Todd played the role of the Rev. Peter Marshall in a highly successful Hollywood film, *A Man Called Peter,* telling the life story of this famous Protestant minister. Fredric March was a Methodist minister in 1941's *One Foot in Heaven* and, in 1950, Joel McCrea portrayed a Protestant evangelist in *Stars in My Crown*. David Niven played the bishop in Samuel Goldwyn's 1947 film, *The Bishop's Wife*. In *The Leather Saint,* John Derek portrayed a young Episcopalian priest.

Two recent landmarks in Hollywood's treatment of religious subjects were Mr. DeMille's twelve-million-dollar production of *The Ten Commandments* and a new Christ portrayal in the Rev. James K. Friedrich's film, *Day of Triumph*. Since DeMille's *King of Kings,* Hollywood has tended to show Christ "only as a shadow, a light, a symbol, a back or a vague outline."[18] The new Christ portrayal, by Robert Wilson, was the first in a major Hollywood release for twenty-seven years. *The Hollywood Reporter* commented about Wilson:

No acting role could possibly be as difficult as that of playing Jesus. Robert Wilson undertakes it and does a remarkably good job. An actor of limited experience, but possessing depth and power, it will be interesting to see where he goes from here.[19]

A British actor, R. Henderson Bland, had portrayed Christ back in 1912 in *From the Manger to the Cross*. He has left behind a most interesting memoir about the day, on location in Palestine, when he was portraying Our Lord on the way to Golgotha:

I shall never forget the day I toiled along the Via Dolorosa with the huge symbol that has carried the message of mercy through the ages. Great crowds stood for hours in the blazing sun and numbers lined the walls and covered the roofs of the houses. The crowds around my carriage were so dense that police were told to keep the people back. When I left the carriage to take up my position in the scene a way was made for me with no word said. Women stepped forward and kissed my robe.[20]

The French film, *Monsieur Vincent,* is a masterpiece among "religious" films. Another film of a religious nature that received general release and critical plaudits is the Louis de Rochemont production of *Martin Luther*. This film well served its purpose of telling the story of the great reformer, managed to be entertaining and, without undue sensationalism, achieved vigorous action and lively portrayals of historical characters. Its essential portrayal of adventure was in the realm of ideas rather than physical melodrama, and this surprisingly caught the public's interest.

The mass media mixture of Bible and ballyhoo, not at all surprisingly, has given rise to a somewhat ribald view of the entire situation. For the few more earnest film efforts of an explicitly religious nature, there has been a plenitude of big-budget, extravaganza-like, hotly promoted films dishing up sex, lusty paganism and strange scriptural sentiment in a potpourri. A London reporter caught something of the ribald view of the situation in an interview with the Hollywood actor, Mr. Victor Mature. Mr. Mature was described as "the man who helped make the Bible box office, who slew the Philistines and fought the lions." In the course of the published interview, the reporter asked Mr. Mature if he never found himself short of breath when going up a steep hill.

The Hunk of Man looked hurt. He said cunningly: "Haven't you seen my pictures? Didn't you see me push down those pillars with my own two hands in Samson and Delilah? *Didn't you see me fight the tigers with my bare hands in* Demetrius and the Gladiators?"
"Yes," I said, "but I could probably have pushed down those pillars myself. Under the direction of Cecil B. DeMille."
Mr. Mature grinned. "I guess maybe you could have," he said. Victor Mature is a man of whom it could be said that he was saved by the Bible. Biblical epics like Samson and Delilah *have kept him in the top category of Hollywood stars.*[21]

In addition to the big-budget, major-studio film extravaganzas that are advertised as religious pictures, and also the handful of generally distributed but more modestly budgeted religious film efforts, there are films made for Church use, for instructional and also for evangelical purposes. These are not intended for theatrical distribution.

The greater part of them are made by Christian production organizations. This gives rise to a complex question: What is a *Christian* production organization? If it is "nonprofit" motivated, still it must make money in order to plough money back into increased production. If it is not "commercial," still it must employ talent, make use of advertising and promotion, and compete at a business level with other production organizations within the same category and with some outside of the category. As one finds it difficult to speak of a *Christian* nation or a *Christian* ruler or a *Christian* enterprise—outside of pure theory, and in terms of practice or witness—so one shies away from signalizing a motion-picture production organization that specializes in "religious" or "Christian" films as *Christian.* Did not St. Francis himself, on his deathbed, say to his brethen, "Now let us *begin* to be Christians"? The responsibility of pinning the label of Christian to any essentially business enterprise, even when it has a strand of altruistic or selfless motive, is a heavy one. One would like to be spared the spectacle of a *Christian* film-production organization involved in widely publicized court litigation with an actor who had been signed to portray on the screen Jesus Christ, or St. Paul, or the humble St. Francis of Assisi.

In this category of films, there is the question of story. Will only biblical material be adapted and dramatized, or will "modern" stories be developed, relating, for example, to Christian ethics and everyday problems of life? There is the problem of developing writers for the specialized task of creating such scenarios. A comprehension of more than literal familiarity with the Scriptures is desirable, yet such familiarity is itself to be hailed warmly. Of course, such familiarity alone, without a scenarist's developed skill, will not suffice. Directors must be developed. These must combine the skill of their craft with an understanding of the motivation underlying the production. Casting is a major problem. Who will portray Jesus Christ? The Virgin Mary? St. Paul? What is the professional background of the actors sought? What is their motivation? What of the nature of their private lives, especially from the standpoint of personal publicity now, or later? Many theological questions arise in the treatment of biblical subjects by religious films. The British publication, *Theology,* offered the following remarks concerning the depiction of the resurrected Christ in a singularly honored picture produced for Church distribution, *I Beheld His Glory:*

In his laudable zeal to proclaim the risen Christ the producer tries to make visible what is visible only to faith, and in the Upper Room the Lord speaks to Thomas the words about seeing and believing and does so in the film. After that, we see the stairs outside the Upper Room and the Centurion Cornelius on the stairs. Thomas opens the door to the Roman officer and breathlessly tells him that he has just seen Jesus. Then he says: "Did you not see Him?" "Where?" is the officer's reply. "He must have met you on the stairs," says Thomas. "Yes, yes, His robe must have brushed my arm," the centurion whispers in awe. It may be very moving . . . yet it is offensive. Is everything allowed in a film? Are all means justified by the end? Can we mix up all the events of the New Testament in that fashion? Did He who, according to the witness of St. Luke and St. John, stood in their midst whilst the doors were locked use the stairs? It sounds a silly question, but it has to be asked. Poetic license is one thing, but it must be limited by certain theological considerations. It reveals a complete misunderstanding of the Event of the resurrection to show such a scene and to let a man utter those words.

And turning again to the nonbelieving viewer, will that convince him? Will that help him to believe in the risen Christ? Does not the film, through such a little well-meant addition, make the whole Event a "myth"? And does it not thereby defeat its own purpose? There is . . . dare I say it? . . . something almost ridiculous about this little scene. It seems to make the whole Event cheap and quite incredible. It fastens the viewer's thought not on the Person who has overcome death but rather on his external appearance. It does not *make it more "real." For the reality of the risen Person cannot be described in this way. It only helps to suggest unreality, the one thing which the records deny, a phantasma or ghost.*[22]

A large number of films made for Church use are employed extensively in foreign missionary activity. A letter received by a producer of such films told of one such showing for several hundred natives in a missionary area. Due to the size of the crowd, the film had to be shown in an open-air space. The film was projected onto a cement wall of a village building, which served as the screen. Audio-visual trucks carrying mobile equipment make showings possible in many areas of missionary outreach. Thus, the Gospel is proclaimed in a new and striking way by means of films.

A problem has arisen in the use of Western-produced and Western-oriented religious films in Eastern mission areas. It is a part of the great contemporary problem of basic communication between East and West. An altruistic gesture of sending to the East several dozens of prints of an American-produced biblical film may not be really helpful in the Church's over-all missionary task, and may hinder it. It is increasingly becoming stressed that Christianity, preached by Western missionaries and missionary methods, must not be identified with Western culture. Some experts are suggesting that we encourage native producers of religious films, for example, and seek to replace Western audiovisual materials with those produced within an Eastern cultural milieu. The initiative in such a project would undoubtedly have to come from the West itself. The West is finding that the Eastern Christian needs to develop autonomy in expressing his faith in cultural freedom. The West weighs heavily upon such freedom by the sheer force of cultural, economic and political impact. A poster contest was sponsored for young artists in a section of Africa, in an effort to stimulate the growth of indigenous cultural expression. Yet, in terms of long-range impact, one widely distributed Hollywood film in that area far outweighs such a contest in a comparative effect upon cultural expression. The Rev. H. R. Weber, Director of the Lay Department of the World Council of Churches, deals with this aspect of communication in a new study. He spent four years in central Celebes and Java, and he comments in light of his experiences and resulting insights growing out of evangelization work among illiterates.

"Religious drama," while not a mass medium, strongly influences mass media dealing with Christian subjects. Miss Sayers' *The Zeal of Thy House,* Mr. Eliot's *Murder in the Cathedral* and Christopher Fry's *The Boy With the Cart* are dramas in a "religious" setting, dealing with characters who are involved in tension and decision which is of a recognizable religious nature. Mr. Eliot's *The Cocktail Party* and Mr. Fry's *The Dark Is Light Enough* are equally "religious drama," yet many a Broadway or London theatregoer has completely missed the point of each. Such theatregoers have been aware that a definite "message" was involved, but could not state it, and they have probably not really had a very good time in the bargain. Here, if I may say so, is a more sophisticated example of the crisis in Christian communication.

IMPLICIT CHRISTIAN COMMUNICATION

There is a story, which may well be apocryphal, concerning Noel Coward and an actress friend of his. She is reported to have accepted

Mr. Coward's invitation to attend, as his guest, a London theatre performance, with these words: "If it's a play with a message, I won't dress." Of course, any play Mr. Coward could have taken her to see in London that night, be it a musical, a light comedy or a serious drama, had a message. There is not a play or TV program or film or magazine or comic strip extant that does not have a message.

All media of communication are theological. Christoph Blumhardt, a German pastor, saw the connection back in 1850 between the Bible and the newspaper—between *this* and *that* in Christ. He brought together the men of his church one night each week. One week they would read the Bible together. The next week they would read the newspaper together, interpreting it in light of God's action in history and in terms of man's sin in politics and other spheres of life.

We must deal with the question: What is a "religious" medium of mass communication? What, exactly, is a "religious" film or television program or magazine? A work of art, as a very encounter of faith, may leave us caught up into what a writer has described as

an unforgettable intensity of life . . . haunted forever with the sense of vast dignities and strange sorrows and teased with thoughts beyond the reaches of our souls.[23]

Of *Hamlet,* the same writer has written:

Its true hero is man . . . haunted man . . . man with his mind on the frontier of two worlds, man unable either quite to reject or quite to admit the supernatural, man struggling to get something done as man has struggled from the beginning, yet incapable of achievement because of his inability to understand either himself or his fellows or the real quality of the universe which has produced him.[24]

Let us examine the relationship between Christian faith and creative work that is not explicitly Christian. This relationship is found, for example, when we start dealing with situations wherein creative people are not aware of the impression they are hammering out with a very telling effect upon others. This impression, actually, may be the very opposite of that intended by the creative artist. A creative person may simply write a film scenario about people and things; he has no realized Christian concept at all, and, in fact, may disclaim the existence of God. Yet such a writer's finished product is of intense interest to us because, without realizing it, he is dealing with

God, with man, with sin, with the Incarnation and Atonement: one always deals with these, one way or the other.

Regard the art form of the motion picture. From the first films of Griffith, Ince and other pioneers to the best current product of Huston, Wyler and Stevens, theology is woven through the films as a thread through tapestry. It is equally interesting when the artists are aware of it, and when they are not. God remains everlastingly God, man is man, sin is sin.

The best work of art (and we are still discussing the specific art form of the motion picture) manages whether consciously or unconsciously to achieve integrity in perspective. God is at the hub of His world. If man is placed fictionally at the hub, and is made to attempt to manipulate the forces of life which we know by experience he cannot successfully manipulate, we automatically have set in motion a situation that must resolve itself in either destruction (isolation) or repentance. You may be familiar with C. S. Lewis' book, *The Great Divorce,* which tells of a bus that leaves hell, every hour, on the hour, for heaven. A queue forms and a number of persons make the trip; but they return. They do not want heaven, they do not see heaven as heaven: fundamentally, a change must take place first within them before they can see it, or see it as heaven. After all, heaven is a place where God is glorified, and these persons are too egocentrically motivated to want to be with God or to glorify Him. I think of the ship that sails out of the bay in Hawaii at the conclusion of James Jones' novel (and, later, screen play) *From Here to Eternity.* The two women standing together on its deck are really going nowhere; they are rooted in their separation from God, they are slaves of themselves, they are in hell. A boat pulls out of a Hawaiian harbor in James Jones' novel, as a bus pulls out of hell in C. S. Lewis' book—but does the state of mind change? God knows, it can; but do these two women in the Jones story, and do the passengers on Lewis' bus, desire such a change? Do they repent?

A medium of communication certainly possesses an implicit religious meaning if it realistically mirrors the human condition, if it offers an insight into a human soul alienated from God. A medium of communication need not mention "sin" or "man" or "God" in an explicit way in order to do so in an implicit way. Simply adding God the Father to the star roster of a motion picture, and including ministerial associations in advance promotion plans, does not per se make a film "religious"! In doing extensive research on the subject of various self-styled "religious" motion pictures, one is shocked to find so much shiny "religious" surface for so much heightened money-making motivation under the guise of spiritual altruism.

There is no explicit doctrine of man in the vast majority of films. But there is certainly a recognizable Christian doctrine of man, which is implicit, which is stated in "negative witness" and which in just that kind of a statement is far more graphic, far more powerful when converted into positive witness. "Negative witness" is what Pastor Exbrayat of France calls Jean Paul Sartre's play, *Huis Clos:* "A negative witness, simple, dynamic, and in colloquial language."[25] He chooses this particular work as "Christian evangelizing" because, by Christian interpretation of what is explicitly an atheistic statement, we can see the Faith so clearly.

Negative witness is asserted indirectly; it has an implicit Christian significance that needs to be excavated. And, for such a task, we need the tools of Christian discrimination; and this brings us to the door of theology. This is a most challenging way of bringing a large number of laymen and laywomen to the door of theology, too. Many novels, films, magazine stories and articles, newspaper reports, TV and radio programs are concerned, in a dramatic and compelling way, with our real human condition, with the crisis that man is sensing in living today. Amos Wilder comments on this, saying that man's present crises—political, social, cultural, psychological—are so fateful and destructive because they are compounded with a deeper crisis, an existential crisis, a crisis of man's deepest self.

> *What, again, is this deeper crisis? The language used with regard to it sounds melodramatic, but points to the truth. We are all familiar with expressions of Paul Tillich. He speaks of the "sense of the abyss." He speaks of the "shaking of the foundations." Others speak of nihilism: that is, the loss of roots in modern culture, the solvent actions of positivistic science, the dehumanization of our economic order, have brought man face to face with nothingness, and so with certain experiences of vertigo, horror, nausea, estrangement. Even where the predicament is not felt at its most acute, there is a widespread sense of anxiety, and Auden speaks of the "Age of Anxiety."*[26]

This observer calls for Christians to be aware of, and to achieve some identification with, "the wrestling with evil that is going on in the deeper culture of our time." He characterizes the period as one of "spiritual gestation" and, noting how the secular world has been forced to identify the spiritual resources needed for survival, calls the major works of contemporary literature "undeniably theological in character."[27]

The underlying character of the persons in our novels, plays, TV–radio dramas and films, lends itself to theological interpretation of the most significant kind. One is immediately concerned with anthropology, with the ontological question, with the creation and the fall and the redemptive work of God in Christ. In the film *Country Girl,* for example, Bing Crosby tries despairingly to justify himself, while at the same time fighting with all his might against the fact of his justification lying outside of himself, that is, only in Christ. This was never *said;* the film bore no "religious" markings; not more than one out of a hundred persons who saw the film even considered that there might be an iceberg of Christian relevance underneath its slick surface. In *Citizen Kane,* we see the hazy outline of, at best, a partial knowledge of self. We see, too, the rejection of self-acceptance. The mystery of *this* "person," this Citizen Kane, was to be fought, rationalized, acknowledged briefly in broken and illogical (to observers) moments of desperation, and finally wrestled with upon an ornate and gaudy deathbed. There is meaningful symbolism (a sleigh in some snow, somewhere, or a name of absolutely private meaning like the "Rosebud" of *Citizen Kane*) in every man's life. Do we accept, even seek, or do we reject the symbolism in our own lives? Is our own person to be accepted, as having been created in the image of God and planted on earth in a certain time and at a certain place; or is our own person to be seen as wholly self-developed? Will we "break" ourselves and "make" ourselves in our own or Satan's image, or will we dig in both earthy and heavenly soil for the roots that may tell us who we are? Pathetic self-justification and buoyed-up self-importance, and a failure of honest self-acceptance, were the basic factors in William Holden's character in the motion picture *Picnic.* Only by seeing and accepting himself (and by being accepted by someone else) could he desire amendment and a change in the direction of his life. Such a desire would be a necessary step before the change itself could slowly take place.

I remember seeing, in England, the French film based on the Colette novel *Le Blé en Herbe.* It was shown in the United States as *The Game of Love.* The local newspaper advertisment was headlined: "See it and discuss it in whispers." The film's classification was "X"; no person under 16, accompanied or not, could be admitted to any part of the program. The audience reacted as it had been prepared by the mass media to react. One heard snickers during delicate scenes, one heard bawdy laughter in scenes of emotional violence. The film itself is honest and an effective study of adolescence and human loneliness and sexual hunger. Its theme is universal. The film captures poignantly the lost wonder, the meaninglessness, in giving of one's body, and perhaps of one's personality, to another personality for just an isolated moment without significance for the years and for eternity. One thinks of Eden as the camera follows the two young persons walking together along the grey, colorless seashore. Will they marry? (What of the *sacrament?*) *Why* should they marry, except that she is now naked and unprotected and needs this other human being, and that he is caught in a pattern without which a larger pattern would not make sense? And what is life but a pattern? "Christ, what are patterns for?"

The stage play by Terence Rattigan, *Separate Tables,* employs the imagery of separate tables in a hotel restaurant to depict, in a devastating way, human loneliness and isolation. Often such a "negative witness," discerned, interpreted and changed into positive witness, will do more to confront a non-Christian with the Gospel than anything else can do. In other words, nonreligious drama (or film, or television, for example) may convey implicit Christian truth more significantly for some persons than "religious" drama could do, for the latter might only stiffen a non-Christian's initial attitude of indifference, resentment or downright opposition. New signs of interest in Christian thought among intellectuals seem to be induced not so much by theological writing as by plays, music, pictures, novels and poetry. "It is often in the theatre that a sense of responsibility for religious issues is highly developed." [28]

In Holland, the cinema and the theatre have, for large sections of the population, become substitutes for the Church, as they are "places where it is still possible to see real personalities, whom one can no longer meet anywhere else.[29] In Groningen, selected films have been shown by the churches in large cinemas, and these have constituted the basis of sermons in follow-up church services. It has been discovered that a film that is not "Christian" nevertheless "may fulfill an important function by opening people's eyes to life, bringing up real questions and showing the real frontiers, and thus making people reflect." [30] In Scotland, art as *praeparatio evangelica* among intellectuals has been widely hailed as being in terms of identifiable intellectual and moral problems.

It touches their life. It states their problems, even if it does not solve them. It offers some light and shows some touch of glory in the life they are living.[31]

J. B. Priestley, in a few words, offer us an excellent definition of hell in terms of "negative witness":

Hell—not fiery and romantic but grey, greasy, dismal—is just around the corner.[32]

Vittorio De Sica's great film, *Umberto D,* concerns an old man in Italy, his dog, desperately bad economic conditions, and a young woman who is pregnant but does not know which one of the two lovers she has taken is her baby's father. How does De Sica describe the meaning of this film? "It seeks to put on the screen the drama of man's inability to communicate with his fellow man," he has explained

When everything is at a dead end, when there is no more hope of getting help from anybody, it is just then that Umberto could have found a way out. By taking the girl out of this house, being a father to her. Two or three, together might solve their problems. Nothing of this sort happened. Human beings have this primitive, perennial, ancient fault of not understanding one another, of not communicating with each other. This is the story of "Umberto D," that is to say, of a man like ourselves.[33]

In our consideration of any film, in the light of the free wills of men, we are face to face with fascinating possibilities. Given clay, what will man A choose to mould? Given film and sound equipment, what will man B try to translate into a finished work of art for a mass audience? There is freedom for these creators, the only limitation being in terms of technical craftsmanship, materials, social pressures (in the guilt of which they share) and their own misuse of freedom. The purpose? Man is free to see God's creation as a unity or to see it in broken fragments, and, indeed, to see God in His creation not at all. The creator—in this case, the maker of motion pictures (the producer, director, writer, or combination of two or all three of these functions)—may, for example, deny the existence of sin or acknowledge it. Yet he is dealing with it; it exists in life.

Do the characters in a particular film ring true? Are these real people up there on the screen, or just "stars" walking through the paces of another "vehicle"? For persons to be real, even on the screen, motivation must be honest. There are certain basic factors in the human condition and in the Divine Revelation. These are in operation in a theological seminary in Paris; in a factory outside of Kansas City; and also on a sound stage or in a producer's office on a movie lot in Hollywood. In a given film, we see characters first on the surface of their lives. But, always, we see persons initially in this way, barring meeting under a cataclysmic circumstance that tears away the layers of self-protection. The surface view, as we know of others and as others know of us, may be maddeningly different from the inner nature. There is a reality in each. There is, first, the essential nature of human personality and of a human personality. And, too, there is the modification and development of the essential nature under the pressures of society and as the result of many, and often conflicting, motivations, tensions and decisions. Up there on the screen, do we see any of this "life process"—or does it remain just surface? Do we come face to face with sin and its consequences? Undoubtedly we do, though the creator or creators of the film may be quite unaware of this.

Positive witness is asserted through direct means, of course; and through the direct means of converting negative witness, of bringing to light its implicit meaning. In positive witness, an explicit meaning is present. Generally, as we know, we are dealing in mass media with negative, rather than with positive, witness. All films, as we have said before, are theological; but some are enchantment, some are honest. All may bear a negative witness, but the honest ones (and those, too, that one would never be apt in a superficial way to associate with religion, such as *A Streetcar Named Desire*) are "in spirit and in truth." I believe they are perhaps nearer the Kingdom of God than some self-styled "religious" pictures that merely exploit the media of mass communication. Sherman E. Johnson made the comment:

"The plays of Sophocles and Aeschylus are as important as Job; a movie like The Ox-Bow Incident *has something to say."* [34]

A film or periodical or television show or radio program, if it is honest in spirit and in truth, gives us an element of life. Activity along the lines of Christian interpretation, translating into Christian terms what is right before one's eyes in life, is of the utmost importance in what we call "Christian Education" if there are to be more Christians and if all of us are to be educated as Christians living in today's world, which is where we happen to live and where Christ finds us. The Christian expression in any medium of communication is that which is essentially honest, and, because its portrayal of character and event is true, enables us to perceive the Person of Christ and His work and significance for us and for our everyday lives.

"Negative witness" in popular songs would, in itself, provide a meaty theme for dissertation. Such songs speak to the deep feelings of millions of men and women who identify such feelings with them. Often there is no "answer" to problems, only identification with expressions of problems and moods. Through juke boxes, car radios, home radio sets and various other channels of mass communication, a popular "hit" song is dinned into the ears of millions of persons. One song preaches explicitly what so many others only preach implicitly, that we are to "dream." Another song is a classical preachment of our century about "love." It is inherent within this song that love is a binge of unparalled abandon, that binge follows binge, and that each one is different from the other and earnestly to be sought. It is good to be hurt, we are told, and one is, each time, hurt in a different way. Eventually one may, as a veteran, sip one's ale in little inns and play the juke boxes and identify one's binges and hurts with popular songs. Popular songs possess a theological significance of the first magnitude within our society. They offer laments, ecstasy, chronicles of hurts and escapes and escapes and escapes. The ultimate irony seems to be that a person enchanted by just such techniques of communication often spurns the Church "because it is just an escape." Escape from what, into what, into Whom? One never "escapes" into Christ, even into His Wounds. In this connection it behooves us to notice a distinction that Brother George Every set down with considerable insight:

A distinction ought to be made between religious art and art on religious subjects. The poetry of the fifteenth-century French poet Villon has been called extremely religious, though he himself was a sad scamp; and we can speak of the deeply religious outlook implied in James Joyce's Ulysses, *which was for some time officially unprintable. In such a case we mean that the work implies an outlook of life which is religious and not humanist, which recognizes, as the great religious traditions recognize, the weakness and sinfulness of man, and his need for redemption. But art which is not in this sense religious may very well be about religion, for religion, love, and nature are the three perennial subjects of poetry, painting, and sculpture.*[35]

Real Christianity is never an escape from life; but no amount of "religious" subjects will make escape art Christian.

We must note, also, another subtle distinction of the utmost importance. There may be an implicit meaning within a medium of communication intended to convey an explicit meaning, and this implicit meaning may be absolutely contradictory to the desired explicit meaning. In our age of mass communication, when a mounting babel of "communication" is in fast progress, the danger is magnified of our actually communicating the opposite of what is intended. An explicitly "religious" medium of mass communication may carry within itself an implicit refutation of its own claim. For example, the exploitation of sex and profligacy in *Samson and Delilah* negated the true context of the Biblical content.

Another example may be cited. *David and Bathsheba* dealt with biblical characters and was described by many critics as a "biblical epic." Yet its implicit appeal to movie-goers was in terms of its identification with the star system and of its spicy exploitation of a particular sensual incident in David's life, his act of adultery with the wife of Uriah the Hittite. Another example may be cited from a "religious" film made for Church use. An incident from the life of Christ was being portrayed in the film. Yet a single close-up of Jesus, at the conclusion of the film, was so phony that it preached the exact opposite of what the producer intended to preach through the medium of the film. The close-up revealed a precious, unreal, embarrassingly coy Jesus, eyes turned toward "heaven," smilingly utterly removed from "earth." The close-up was antithetical to the words of the Nicene Creed: "Who for us men and for our salvation came down from heaven, And was incarnate by the Holy Ghost of the Virgin Mary, And was made man: And was crucified also for us under Pontius Pilate, He suffered and was buried." Jesus Christ became *human* as well as being divine. He took upon Himself, for our salvation, our very humanity. A film based on Jesus' life, or on an incident in it, that implicitly negates the core of the entire Gospel message is involved in the saddest and most profound of self-contradictions.

Film Daily recently carried a story about a new "multimillion dollar production, *The Son of Man,* based on the life of Christ."[36] This may well be a "religious" or even a Christian film, but it may well be neither. We cannot yet judge its subject matter; it is more important to see what its motivation shows, and whether this Christ is indeed the Son of God and real man or whether He is a pharisaical sentimentalist with an emasculated message to proclaim. At its simplest level, we fall into the plight of the preacher to whom was said: "What you are speaks so loudly that I cannot hear what you are saying." This matter is made infinitely more complex by the advent on the scene of television, radio, films, mass publications and so forth. A man, by what he is, may now speak so loudly that millions of persons will receive this "communication" instantaneously, and not hear what he is saying. On the other hand, an event, televised widely, may speak with an undying significance and make a burning imprint upon public consciousness. This is honesty, and this is to be sought from a Christian standpoint; yet many will shrink from it, and many Christians will shrink from it, too, when the weakness and particular failure of the Church is thus mercilessly and surgically exposed by the Church itself.

Today many quite "sincere" persons using media of mass communication for "religious" or "Christian" presentations are merely sentimental. However, within the area of various media that have no expressed idea of being religious, or interest in being Christian, we find the deep questions concerning the human situation coming to the surface. A major task of the Church is to perceive clearly this "negative witness" in so much of contemporary creative expression, and to point the way towards converting that very negative witness into a positive Christian witness. The theatre, novel, film, radio play, television program, popular song, comic strip, magazine or newspaper has often become far more effective today than the pulpit in expressing man's realistic condition, in giving voice to questions that man asks within his own soul. The Church needs to thank these media for such honest and effective expression of man's questions; and then the Church needs to convey to man the answer of God's revelation of Himself in Jesus Christ, and what this means to man as he pursues his everyday life in a complex world that he little understands.

FOOTNOTES FOR RELIGIOUS COMMUNICATION BY MASS MEDIA

[1] Brother George Every, *Christian Discrimination,* p. 8.
[2] *Evanston Speaks,* op. cit., pp. 37–8.
[3] Martin Jarrett-Kerr, C. R., "A Saint On The Threshold," *The Frontier,* p. 30, Jan., 1951.
[4] Dorothy L. Sayers, *The Man Born To Be King,* p. 20.
[5] Everett C. Parker, David W. Barry, Dallas W. Smythe, *The Television-Radio Audience and Religion,* pp. 109–11.
[6] *Ibid.,* p. 397.
[7] Francis H. House, "Religious Broadcasting," *A Christian Year Book,* p. 133.
[8] "In Review," *Broadcasting-Telecasting,* p. 14.
[9] *Radio Daily,* March 2, 1955.
[10] Vernon Sproxton, *Watching Films,* p. 19.
[11] *The Moving Picture World,* p. 233, Oct. 19, 1912.
[12] R. E. Sherwood, *Literary Digest,* p. 29, Feb. 6, 1926.
[13] *Variety,* p. 38, Jan. 6, 1926.
[14] Cecil B. DeMille, "Memoirs," Los Angeles *Examiner,* p. 3, Dec. 24, 1950.
[15] *Variety,* p. 14, Dec. 6, 1932.
[16] Van A. Harvey, "Pageantry and Relics," *Episcopal Churchnews,* p. 26, March 6, 1955.
[17] Gilbert Seldes, *The Great Audience,* p. 96.
[18] "Too Concrete?," *Time,* p. 87, Oct. 11, 1948.
[19] *The Hollywood Reporter,* p. 4, Dec. 1, 1954.
[20] Ernest A. Dench, *Making the Movies,* p. 79.
[21] Thomas Wiseman, "Mr. Mature Is Just a Trifle Nervous," London *Evening Standard,* p. 6, June 18, 1955.
[22] Ernest Gordon, *"I Beheld His Glory,"* Theology, p. 46, Feb., 1954.
[23] C. S. Lewis, "Hamlet: The Prince or the Poem?," Annual Shakespeare Lecture of the British Academy 1942, *From the Proceedings of the British Academy,* Vol. XXVIII.
[24] *Ibid.*
[25] *Evangelism in France,* p. 21.
[26] Amos N. Wilder, *Modern Poetry and the Christian Tradition: A Study in the Relation of Christianity to Culture,* pp. 207–8.
[27] *Ibid.,* p. xiii.
[28] *Evangelism—The Mission of the Church to Those Outside Her Life, op. cit.,* p. 25.
[29] *Evangelism in Holland,* p. 20.
[30] *Ibid.,* p. 21.
[31] *Evangelism in Scotland,* p. 25.
[32] J. B. Priestley, "The World of the Novel—Cops & Robbers," London *Sunday Times,* Nov. 21, 1954.
[33] Vittorio De Sica, "Analyzing 'Umberto'," New York *Times,* p. 15, Oct. 30, 1955.
[34] Malcolm Boyd, "All Films Are Theological," *The Christian Century,* p. 1457, Dec. 1, 1954.
[35] Brother George Every, *op. cit.,* p. 20.
[36] *Film Daily,* p. 6, March 1, 1956.

POINT
OF CONTACT

INTRODUCTION The communicator must be involved with three things: the message he is trying to establish, the method of communication, and the person to whom he is reaching out and with whom he must find a "point of contact."

The problem of our finding a "point of contact" for our proclamation of the Gospel is a crucial one. Hendrik Kraemer points to the spiritual atomization of our present world and to the fact that unity of culture is broken, referring to the great upsurge in autonomous thinking and the shattering of age-old life patterns by the industrial and technical revolution (and the results of this, including the growth of secularization, and urbanization with its conglomeration of people atomized in their relationships).[1]

What do men today understand by Christianity? Sydney Cave advances a disturbing answer:

There was a time when men rejected Christianity because they disbelieved in miracles or in the Divinity of Christ. In our age a commoner cause is this: what they understand by Christianity has been disproved by their experience of life.[2]

The Church is not communicating adequately with a society that wants the hard answers, but does not want them enough to push aside the "fluff" and the easy answers when these are offered instead. Instead of dialogue between the Church and persons in society, too often there is only monologue in misunderstanding and mutual quiet desperation. This can be compared with a cocktail party "conversation" between two persons who are talking to one another, but only in overlapping monologues, for relationship has not been established. The monologues are isolated and without connection.

Our distortion of the Word of God and our failure to interpret the Sacraments in a meaningful way for the churched as well as for the unchurched are both parts of the crisis in Christian communication.

"Do you ever consider what God's purpose is for you, why He created you and what He would like you to do with your life?" This question was asked of a twenty-nine-year-old man, an account executive for one of the leading advertising agencies in the United States. He answered: "I do not think of God as having a vocational purpose for me. I imagine ministers, doctors, teachers, etc., feel this . . . but I doubt if business people do."

"How active are you in your church and what is the relation of your church life to the rest of your life?" This question was asked of a thirty-one-year-old man, a junior partner in a law firm. He replied: "I am becoming increasingly active in my faith and have every intention of offering time to the church if and when the time and need arises. By 'need' I mean when the church feels that I can offer something."

And yet, it is explicitly stated in the life of the Church that we do offer Something: the very Person of Jesus Christ to God the Father in the only Holy and Acceptable Sacrifice. And, through the action of Christ, we are enabled to offer God our hearts and souls and mind, in an offering of love we would not be enabled to make except in, and through, Him.

WHERE IS THE POINT OF CONTACT?

The crisis in our trying to find "point of contact" in Christian communication is deeply complex. How shall we communicate? Some talk simply of the necessity to "preach" the Gospel, on the actual level of semantics; others talk of "preaching," assuming that the preacher possesses a world view, a cultural understanding, a psychological perception and, of course, a sound grasp of Gospel content and meaning. Many believe sincerely that the life of Christ, expressed liturgically and pastorally, is quite sufficient witness in the world. Some, very rightly, remind us that Christian communication consists of listening as well as speaking. Others, driven by frustration and by a compulsion to relate the life of the Church to every—or to some—other area of life, often disappear into side roads or new concepts or methodology labeled *"avant garde."* Many believe the greatest, and, in the final analysis, the only effective witness to the world is the "Christian life." The French Jesuit, Jean Danielou, has noted that "Christianity is essentially a *life,* and not essentially a philosophy. For us, to be Christian is to live divinely, that is, to have grace within us and to have intimacy with God."[3] The "Christian life" is actually an action of God rather than of man, it is appropriated by man with faith and thanksgiving, it becomes a process by grace of sanctification in this life and beyond it. As a mere verbal description, it seems almost too abstract, almost too inextricably a part of process. It is poised on a brink of self-righteousness, for, in earnestly desiring "holiness," we must not fail to involve ourselves wholeheartedly and faithfully in the lives and affairs of our brother human beings. Consider the earthiness of the art of Pieter Breughel as evidenced in such a painting as his Nativity Scene: this reminds us that God became *man* to dwell among *men,* for our salvation. Art becomes guilty of Monophysite leanings when it intrudes upon the angelic territory by depicting men as angels in their relation to God and to other men. It is in respect to *the place where we are,* to our real condition, that Christ has redeemed us and that God the Holy Spirit sanctifies us to whatever degree that we, with our God-given free wills, permit Him. The paradoxical character of the "Christian life" is an unceasing challenge to us.

Certainly, "total commitment" to God will always involve a falling down and, by God's grace, a getting up again, and a closing ranks with the Christian pilgrimage once more. Edward, in *The Cocktail Party,* speaks of every moment as "a fresh beginning" and life as "only keeping on." Then, he says, "Somehow, these two ideas seem to fit together."[4] This universal aspect of "justification" and "sanctification" is part of the paradox of the "Christian life." Christian communication is not advanced by a too-easy use of words so heavily laden with intrinsic meaning as "Christian life." Seemingly, there is, at best, only partial communication by means of this channel of grace; however, who may know and judge of the working of a specific channel of grace? Generally, we may say that there are many Christian saints sharing with us this pilgrimage of life. However, we must add an important qualification. They are saints *in the making*. They are saints in the process of true oblation, in the crucible, and being wonderfully and fearfully formed for an eternity in the blessed Holy Presence.

We use words to "communicate." Yet society today offers us the picture of confusing barriers of words. Each trade, art and profession develops its own jargon. Paradoxically and ironically, there is a "language of the Church"; yet the Church has a mission to proclaim the Word of God, understandably and faithfully, to all men. Even within the Church itself, there are further word barriers. There are specific words for liturgiologists, biblical scholars, theologians, historians and specialists of various kinds (increasing continuously) who are engaged in relating the life of the Church to other streams of human life. Between the Church and the world (if one may speak so naively of a complex area of overlapping and still undiscovered barriers) there should be a balance between the degree to which the Church can adapt its speech to the world's understanding and the point where the world needs to learn and understand the beauty and meaning of the Church's traditional language. How long, in fact, will it be possible to speak in such simple terms of maintaining such a balance? Will the Church soon find it necessary to speak to the various other specialized groups both in their own words and in the Church's words, on several different levels of understanding simultaneously?

To whom are we communicating, or trying to communicate, the Gospel? There can be no more complex question; the answer is so complex as to defy systematization. Brother George Every stated:

If we were speaking to ears which had never heard of Christianity, the situation might be different; but we must face the fact that today the greater part of our people have met the Scriptures in a vulgarized and sentimentalized form in the course of their secular education. The images have become identified with a sickly sentimental moralism which has nothing to do with the traditional orthodox religious attitude.[5]

The World Council of Churches, in a series of articles about evangelism in various countries, gives us a clear report of how modern man has grown away from the Church, how "inaccessible" he has become, how fundamentally communication lines have been blocked or completely severed. From England has come a shocking reference to "children who do not know the meaning of Christmas, men and women to whom the name of Christ is only a swear-word."[6] Obviously, we are not to envision a Christian people to whom we are speaking a message of reminder about a message they know. St. Paul, in Acts 17, gave his talk to the Athenian philosophers. The philosophers heard and refused; but at least they had met, at least they had heard. We must enable the Gospel to be *heard* today.

We speak of the decision, the choice, a man must make when confronted by the Christian Gospel. It seems that we should consider whether a man is able to make a *free choice*. Is his choice made, after he has a clear comprehension of the Christian life and the Christian Church? Or must he make his choice as a post-Christian, a Christian illiterate? Hendrik Kraemer forcefully has pointed out that the Christian world is enchanted by secularized thinking, and this without any exceptions. Professor Kraemer's reiteration of this basic fact is of the utmost importance. Christians must "disenchant" themselves from creeping secularism. This is a task confronting Christians both for themselves and for the society in which they live. Now, take the case of a man who is post-Christian or a Christian illiterate. Does he not have, first, to be "disenchanted" before he can possibly make a free choice about his life on the basis of objective decision? Surely, grace is inextricably and predominantly involved in his decision; but so is his own free will, responding to God's grace.

We need to understand theologically the import of what has happened to us technologically. We have been brought close together by modern implements and techniques. We are, in fact, physically closer together than ever before in the history of the world. We have found that though we speak our diverse jargons, we share the same wordless language of self-interest, self-assertion and exploitation. So the barriers of "words" are superimposed on the more essential barrier of the breakdown of "understanding," since we are fallen men. We are estranged from God. We are in rebellion against His will for us and for the whole of His world. There is a basic conflict in our nature, and we are therefore even at war with that other side of the conflict within ourselves.

It is this fact that is ignored in a statement by Sylvester L. Weaver, despite its other merits. He rightly sees television as performing a vital service in bringing together different people of the world in different parts of the world.

Think of the working N.B.C. communications center with a thousand monitors being on tap and all your information coming in . . . live, film, and recorded, et cetera . . . edited, indexed, collated, cross-indexed, and the index operated cybernetically with electronic push buttons, so that you can get the stuff just like that *when you want it! You know. Something happens in Athens.* Boing! *The guy pushes the button "Athens," and the lights begin to blink all over the place as Athens starts pouring in.*[7]

One realizes that Mr. Weaver's idea is to the effect that *his* push button may keep a perverted adolescent in a dictator's chair from pushing the possibly fatal button to blow up a part of the world. Enlightenment in togetherness should be as plausible a weapon as any in this fast-paced world to upset the plans of all totalitarian-minded men who thrive on misinformation, secrecy, surprise tactics and lies. Lies are confounded by truth. The veil of secrecy shielding perverse propaganda should be able to be rent by objective facts hammered home. However, in a society marked by the incredible power of push buttons and machines, whom may we trust to determine "truth"? Who shall be objective, without being relative, in determining it? Above all, we should be realistic about man, about ourselves. We need perhaps less demythologizing of the New Testament and more demythologizing of our picture of ourselves. Man's tendency to exploit is a natural concomitant of the moral ambiguity in his basic tension. Reinhold Niebuhr succinctly states: "Man is mortal. That is his fate. Man pretends not to be mortal. That is his sin." [8] If all men were "good," if men did not represent such conflicting tendencies and confounding ambiguities within themselves, it would be a good thing to have Athens "pour in," to be very close—after the pushing of a button—to the Athenians and to all peoples. Considering man as he is, such closeness seems to represent the building of a new Babel: no longer a tower to storm the heavens, but a sprawling, California-style bungalow edifice to extend out vertically, to storm men's minds and souls. A man pushing a powerful enough button to permit Athens to "pour in" may turn out to be a "Big Brother." Big Brother may be "sincere" or he may be "insincere," but he is still Big Brother. The answer to our deep loneliness, to our estrangement from other individuals and cultures, lies not in machines to bring us close enough for psychological annihilation. The answer lies in man's recognition of his actual condition as a sinner, and in his responding to the work that God in Christ has done to save man, just as he is, as a sinner. Unless man understands himself, and his brother, he will use machines to destroy himself and his brother. Man, denying his true nature as a child of God, is not only a sinful creature, but one who continues to withstand the redemptive work done for him by Jesus Christ.

EXPERIMENTS IN POINT OF CONTACT

During 1954–55, I spent considerable time studying at first hand various experiments in establishing "point of contact" for Christian communication in Britain and in Europe. I have attempted to relate these experiments to the main stream of Christian communication which is the vital concern of the Church. The Church has often failed to establish such a point of contact, so it is encouraging and instructive to study these experiments, even when they are not in the field of mass media. Some experiments have to do with mass media, some specifically with working men or intellectuals or a professional group within society (for example, doctors). Some attempt to cut a wide swath across a total parish area. The "house-church" fits into the latter category.

The parish of St. Wilfrid's in Halton, Leeds—in northern, industrial England—comprises some 15,000 persons, including Halton Moor Estate, a slum-clearance area of approximately 6,000 persons. How is the Church going to reach out to these individuals in its very midst; indeed, how is one person within the Church going to be established in acknowledged and effective communication with another person also within the Church itself, so that the reaching out to others may be a corporate act of the body that is the Church? Wrestling with these problems, the vicar, the Rev. Canon E. W. Southcott, started pioneering with what is known as the "house-church."

Early on weekday mornings there are house-church meetings with celebrations of Holy Communion in some of the small houses of the Halton Moor Estate. The lights of the houses break through the cold and blackness outside and testify to the gathering of Christians within for the breaking of bread together—a very effective form of communication, one is told by certain men and women who first observed the goings on from outside, across the street or way, and who are now inside the fold taking part.

The kitchen table is set up in the living room in one of the compact, slum-clearance dwellings. Used candles from the altar at the parish church are placed upon the table that becomes the altar. The vicar has noted the deeper meaning that he has come to experience in saying the words of the service of Holy Communion: "We do not presume to come to this Thy table, O merciful Lord . . . ," when he is celebrating, instead of at the altar in the parish church, at a kitchen table converted into an altar in a house-church of his parish. Homemade bread, the same bread that the family had eaten for tea the night before, is used in the service. The Bible and last evening's newspaper are close together; and they will shortly be in the same conversation, too.

There are three kinds of house-church. One is the intensive house-church, and it is for members who are inside the worshipping community. Another is the extensive house-church, where communicants meet together in the homes of those outside the worshipping fellowship, for example in the homes of lapsed baptized or lapsed communicants, or in the homes of non-Christians (perhaps the families of young couples about to become married). A third kind of house-church is the interdenominational. Speaking of the interdenominational house-church, Canon Southcott has stated:

We cannot build up the Church inside or outside the church building and ignore the fact that there are other places of worship from which we are separated, who gather people for worship, who organize their life and witness quite apart from each other. I believe we cannot go on doing this without ignoring Christ. Canon Oliver Tomkins at the Lund Conference challenged all of us when he said that we must do together everything except those things which we must according to conscience do separately. This approach to the scandal of our unhappy divisions is unknown in the ordinary parish. . . . I believe that at the house level we are next-door to the Ecumenical conversation.[9]

The house-church, which has been gradually developing and taking form in Halton, is seen by the vicar as the answer to prayers said over the past ten years by the parish church for the parish—street by street. A special use of the house-church has been found for children. The Holy Communion vessels, the wine and wafers, are brought from the parish church. First the table in the house is laid for tea; then the children are shown how one would "lay the table" for the Lord's Supper. "Here is the visual aid, please God, many of them will never forget," Canon Southcott has commented.

The cellular structure of each parish, reflecting exactly the cellular structure of each diocese, is something that has been grievously lost in the modern Church, it is felt in Leeds. Each colony of New Testament Christianity is cited as being "honeycombed with smaller units." There is always stressed the necessity of seeing the parish as an organic whole instead of in terms of collections of individuals and organizations. "We have a wholly wrong, or unbiblical, idea of the house-church if we define it as something which is a halfway stage to the parish church," Canon Southcott has said. "Rather, it is a vital cell within the Body itself, which should be reflecting in microcosm the whole life and activity of the community of the Holy Spirit." Here is an example of "point of contact" found in the home, with the family, including children.

Not far away from Leeds is the industrial city of Sheffield. Too often today the industrial plant is seen to be standing almost completely outside the framework of Christian activity. The Industrial Missioner of Sheffield, Canon E. R. Wickham, has worked for more than ten years within the steel industry, represented in Sheffield by a number of major plants. He stresses that there are only the haziest relics of the meaning of Christianity in about 90 per cent of the general population. He finds there is, among the workingmen in Sheffield, only the vaguest idea of the Bible. And the Church is seen by the men simply in terms of a building run by men called "clergy" who conduct sessions called "services."

The ramifications of the Sheffield innovation are many. The Church's total mission to society undergirds the work of the Mission. Canon Wickham has stated:

The questions crying out today for continuing creative thinking are legion in industry, and the most intractable are those concerned with the social, personal and human factors. It is precisely with such that the Christian faith is about. In a word, that is the basic justification for the Church's concern with industry.[10]

Canon Wickham and his four assistants emphasize the Church's involvement with people in an institutional sense, "with principalities and powers." The Industrial Mission in Sheffield seeks to penetrate the economic and social structure of society in which men live. The missioners regularly visit the steel works in which their work is centered, talking with men at lunch and tea times on the shop floor; conduct special conferences for such divergent groups as foremen, young executives and apprentices; and conduct three-day residential conferences each quarter, specifically on Christianity and Industry, which most of the larger works in Sheffield invite men to attend. Here is "point of contact" found in the industrial setting that is the center of the lives of workingmen. There should also be mentioned the New Pilgrim Players, professional company of the Religious Drama Society, who have set up tours throughout England. These actors have presented a twenty-minute play for industrial workers at lunch-time periods. An incident at work has been depicted, with the players costumed as workers. There may be no scenery; the action takes place on the shop or plant floor. The first player, with a cup of coffee in his hand, may just wander in and thereby start off the presentation. Trade union co-operation is required for this kind of dramatic activity.

Canon Wickham says that, if modern industrial life is to be healthy, there are Christian elements that modern society must appropriate. He affirms that men must solve their own problems but points out that "Christianity offers principles which need to be translated into quite technical industrial terms." Fundamental questions are being dealt with in Sheffield: What is Christianity in relationship to justice on the shop floor? To a feeling of responsibility as a worker? What is Christianity in relation to an esteem and high understanding of work itself?

"We are exploring what Christianity demands of our modern industrial order," Canon Wickham states. "There used to be too few jobs and too many men; now there is a need to stimulate drive among men."

Canon Wickham spoke to a group of clergy about the industrial work of the Church, at a conference held at the Willow Grange Conference House, near Sheffield. He mentioned two particular problems facing the Church's mission in industry. First, there was the task of the Christian Church in producing and reproducing itself, generation after generation, in an industrial society. This was the "evangelistic-missionary task." The great mass of manual workers was generally outside the churches, it was reported. In England the loss of churchgoers has followed along carefully ascertainable lines and from very specialized groups of society, principally workers and intellectuals. Secondly, there was the problem arising from the fact that we have not produced a Christian industrialized society commendable to an informed Christian conscience. It was questioned, parenthetically, whether any society merits the adjective "Christian," and it was concluded that one society may be described as "more Christian" or "less Christian" than another.

A radically different approach to Christian communication is found in the Zoë Movement within the Greek Orthodox Church. In Athens I talked with leaders of Zoë and its affiliated movements. There is an urgent demand for the Church in Greece to be as concerned with men in their existential struggle in living and working as with liturgical and ecclesiastical matters. Under Zoë and from this central movement have arisen numerous loosely affiliated groups, including one for nurses, one for doctors, one for university students, one for workingmen, one for intellectuals, one for housewives, to cite a few. The Zoë Movement itself is a monastic community of some hundred priests and laymen, seeking to communicate the Gospel in terms of its relevance to everyday life.

Another major movement is that consisting of the Christian Orthodox Unions. What might be described, in some sense, as a Church countermovement is Apostoliki Diakonia. Here media of communication come into play, too: Apostoliki Diakonia and Zoë have striking new printing presses and issue regular publications, for family reading, for youth, for theologians. The Aktinos Movement, affiliated with Zoë and comprising intellectuals, publishes two periodicals for popular reading which are found on all the kiosks in Athens. Television, radio and film do not yet figure importantly in the scheme of Church renewal and evangelization in Greece. It should be mentioned that the secular press, however, is particularly sensational and exploitative in a way that we sometimes think affects only American papers, and this exerts a profound influence in moulding the social climate in which the Church must exist. The emphasis upon Church renewal as found in the Greek movements is strikingly lay-inspired. Zoë is an assorted mixture of elements: it has a puritan strand, strives to remain solidly within the Church (it stresses, above anything else, the Church's sacramental life), yet attracts large numbers of persons who are both loyal to their faith and dissatisfied with some present conditions in the Church. Here is an attempt to speak to the public without neglecting the Church's language of liturgy and sacrament.

In Paris, Henri de Tienda exercises his ministry in relating the Gospel to the modern film medium. Twelve years ago he noticed that his church in a small French village was not attracting so many people as the local cinema. Now he schedules showings of movies in various meeting places in and near Paris. After the group that has assembled has seen a film, a spirited discussion follows, based entirely upon the picture's Christian significance and its implicit theological message. I attended a showing in Montmartre of *Crime and Punishment*. Afterwards the strangely heterogeneous group talked, under M. de Tienda's chairmanship, for some two hours, relating the dramatic elements of film plot, personalities, conflicts and background to the Christian Gospel. Here negative witness is related to positive witness.

Another novel approach in Christian communication involving mass media is the work in Britain of the Rev. Marcus Morris, who, five years ago, was minister of a parish church and editing only one publication, that being the parish magazine. Today he is editor of four children's comics books topping the peak of British circulation in the comics field. Mr. Morris' activity is important, not simply because of the degree of effective Christian communication he is able to achieve, but because he brings to the comic-book sphere of publishing an altogether Christian concept. Only a small part of Mr. Morris' comics books deal with an explicit Christian teaching, yet the total publishing venture is permeated by Christian insight. Mr. Morris is accomplishing a major task: he is entering into a hitherto almost completely secularized field in a way that commands the respect of the professionals operating in it, and asserting that Christ is involved in it.

One implicit Christian attitude in Mr. Morris' comics concerns the hero figure. He comments on this:

Children identify themselves with the hero. In comics which are harmful for children, the hero almost always wins the day either by brute force or perhaps because he has some magical device which enables him to perform an action which is in fact superhuman. It is a very dangerous thing to suggest to children that there is an easy way out of life, to lead them into the "fantasy of omnipotence." The next step is for the child, or adult, to say: "If only I had a magical device, I could . . ." [11]

Dan Dare in one of Mr. Morris' comics books, *Eagle,* illustrates the implicit Christian point of view characteristic of the editor's comics characters. Dan Dare wins the day, as a hero must, yet through the use of his own abilities and talents. He has courage, common sense and perseverance, and uses modern devices, but none of these is "miraculous."

A second implicit Christian teaching in Mr. Morris' comics concerns social attitude: "Does a strip succeed in showing a child that the way to get on in life is to co-operate with other persons?" Mr. Morris asks. He points out that many strips today teach children to get ahead by cleverly doing in others. His comics teach a Christian social attitude.

Another implicit Christian teaching is in regard to one's attitude toward other races and nationalities. Here Mr. Morris tries not to be strained and overly obvious. Perhaps there is an emphasis to make an Englishman the villain, at least in place of the stereotyped colored foreign person. Mr. Morris points out that "goodness or badness is never a national or racial characteristic" and that "there are both good and bad Arabs."

In choosing the explicit Christian theme in his comics—*to show Christianity in action*—Mr. Morris is motivated by his conviction that children are not so much affected by being preached at as by the effectiveness of seeing Christianity at work. *Eagle* (for boys aged ten to fourteen) recently concluded forty episodes on the life of St. Mark, commencing with his boyhood and extending the narratives through the event of the crucifixion of Christ. The story, prepared by the Rev. Chad Varah, a London vicar, ended with the missionary journeys. On the front cover of *Eagle,* Colonel Frank Dare, drawn by Mr. Morris' artist associate, Frank Hampson, made his comics debut. On the back page of the same issue St. Paul was billed as "The Great Adventurer." Mr. Morris has continued to present his explicit Christian teaching in this manner. *Girl* (for ten- to fourteen-year-old girls) almost always manages to tell the story of a great Christian woman. One series of episodes was about Mary Slessor of Calabar, the missionary to South Africa. Twenty-six weeks of episodes concerned Miriam, the sister of Moses, about whom there are only fourteen references in the Old Testament. The story in *Girl* was really that of Moses as seen from the point of view of his sister, and written to catch the interest of young girl readers. *Robin* (for children learning to read) and *Swift* (for younger brothers of *Eagle* readers) tell Bible stories quite simply, not really in strip form, but combining pictures with texts.

Why are Mr. Morris' comics more often implicitly than explicitly Christian? Because, as he explains, "the Church too often insists on hammering the nail in and saying '*This* is Christian' instead of letting the truth speak for itself."

Controversially, Mr. Morris states his belief that there is nothing at all wrong in ordinary blood-and-thunder literature for children. Children living in our highly mechanized age are out of touch with basic reality, he asserts. He describes "basic reality" as the sea and rivers and the countryside—the simple things that a child needs to express his sense of adventure.

Children want robust and exciting material, and, if they are not given it, will simply look for it elsewhere. All too often we offer children namby-pamby, emasculated material. The fact that they are starved for excitement and adventure is borne out by the popularity of comics. There is nothing at all wrong in ordinary blood-and-thunder. The ordinary cowboy and Indian story does no harm. Actually, there is a considerable danger of well-meaning people who know nothing about children attacking material simply because it contains violence. Chesterton praised honest blood-and-thunder literature as being "as simple as the thunder of heaven and the blood of man." What is wrong with some comics is not that they contain violence, but that they contain only *violence, and also sadism. What is the matter with the majority of children's comics today? Their whole attitude to life. It is a wrong thing for a child to glory in being violent. It is wrong that he should be given macabre and bestial material in comics. . . . However, sooner or later, children must come to terms with life and there is violence in life. If we try to protect a child from that we are doing him a disservice. Why try to say that the world contains only good people doing the right thing?*[12]

A professional child psychologist is given responsibility by Mr. Morris for dealing with special-problem letters that come in the mail from child readers. There is a club that is organized in conjunction with each paper and to which children of that paper's age group belong. The *Eagle* club now has about 100,000 active members. Outings are organized for club members along regional and local lines. Youth hostel trips are run by *Eagle* and *Girl,* tieing in with the Youth Hostel Association. Cricket coaching and football coaching are organized for *Eagle* readers. Each year a series of Christmas carol services is set up by Mr. Morris in several British cathedrals, commencing at St. Paul's, London. There were 9,000 applications to attend the St. Paul's service last Christmas. The cathedral could only accommodate 4,000. Services were also held in Edinburgh, Belfast, Manchester, Bristol, Portsmouth, Birmingham and Cardiff, all during the days immediately preceding Christmas Day. Mr. Morris preaches a short sermon at these services. For acts of heroism or public service by boys and girls, *Eagle* and *Girl* award badges during each week and month. The standard of such awards is kept high, representatives being sent to interview children and their families. The "Eagle of the Year" receives a fortnight's holiday for himself and his family. Unselfishness is one of the most important qualities sought in making these awards.

Mr. Morris has recently also assumed the editorship, for the Hulton Press, of a women's magazine, *House Wife.* There is nothing explicitly Christian in this mass-circulation periodical, but Mr. Morris endeavors to present Christian values in articles on such themes as marriage and child care. Last December he used an article on "The Meaning of Christmas," written by a Christian.

"My function, as I see it, is to try to put over something of what Christianity stands for to people who have either no use for it or else the wrong idea about it, and I must do this in an entirely non-churchy way," the Rev. Marcus Morris told me. "It is not my intention to present in a direct way the doctrines of the Christian faith, but to relate Christian values to ordinary living."

Christian communication in an endeavor to reach the intellectual is considered to be a major part of the Church's task. A unique institution in London, St. Anne's House in Soho, brings together within its walls specialists in academic, cultural and scientific groups and Christians who are literate in regard both to the Gospel and to the fields of specialization. Under the active direction of the Rev. Patrick McLaughlin, St. Anne's House is most vitally concerned with communication. A statement about the future plans of St. Anne's House reads:

We see then that our task for the next five or perhaps ten years is to continue primarily as a centre for research into the vexed problem of communications. Some Western thinkers have recently drawn attention to the diminishing value of words, whether written or spoken, and to a corresponding increase in the value of images. This situation seems to demand a thorough and sustained inquiry into its causes, and the effects upon Western culture of this change from verbal arguments as the sole medium for exchanging ideas to a preoccupation with images, and these mainly visual.[13]

A Guest Night at St. Anne's House had Dorothy L. Sayers and C. S. Lewis discussing Kathleen Nott's controversial book, *The Emperor's Clothes*. In Miss Nott's absence, due to illness, G. S. Fraser, who is on the staff of the *Times Literary Supplement* and talks on the B.B.C. Third Programme in its New Verse series, defended the point of view expounded in her book.

In intellectual, creative approaches, we have either the course of direct exploration (as by the scientist or the poet) or the course of the systematic philosopher and the theologian, Mr. Fraser explained in his talk. Both courses begin at the same point, i.e., "Man is a wretched creature"; but the pragmatic, humanistic course continues in this vein: "Therefore, let him look into the matter and see what he can do about it." Mr. Fraser pointed out that many people of a liberal mind, who had thought of themselves as vestigially Christians and who often irritate practicing and phlegmatic Christians very much, regard Christian dogmas as "blinkers" and "shackles." These people of a liberal mind regard practicing and phlegmatic Christians as "a spiritual elite" playing a little private game, contriving to prove a thesis and letting this process replace the development of life. He referred to Miss Nott's criticism in *The Emperor's Clothes* of the false assumption of superiority by many Christian apologists in fields where they are rank amateurs. The conscious working of Christian dogmas into creative works was cited particularly in the plays of T. S. Eliot. This process, present also in the works of such writers as Miss Sayers and Professor Lewis, is criticized by Miss Nott.

Miss Sayers, during the discussion of Miss Nott's book, said that there is "nothing more fatal to art" than things written with an edifying purpose. However, she went on: "If a Christian has a great experience, then no one has any right to deny him his right to express that experience in his work." She warned, too, that "one must not bolster up scientific truth by falsifying theological truth."

One course of lectures at St. Anne's House under Father McLaughlin's direction, was on the announced subject of "Image, Meaning and Metaphor." The first section consisted of an analysis of communication through language, in natural science, and also as discernible in prolinguistic communication in the natural world and through extrasensory perception. The second group of lectures represented an attempt at a synthesis with the aim of discovering any conclusions that could be drawn in the light of the first inquiry. Eminent artists, philosophers, psychologists and scientists were enlisted as speakers.

A statement from St. Anne's House has this to say about the Church as a communications center in the modern world:

> *It is apparent that the primary need is for the recovery of the prophetic ministry of the Church, recognized and established as an integral part of her operation, alongside the traditional sacramental and pastoral ministries: and for this in turn the outstanding need is for Christians both engaged in ordinary "secular" occupations and trained in a Christian social critique, i.e., in an analysis and interpretation of contemporary history, and particularly of social institutions, which is derived from Biblical revelation.*[14]

St. Catharine's, Cumberland Lodge, located in Windsor Great Park near to London, is an institution that was founded for the specific purpose of offering to staff and students in the universities opportunities to overcome certain contemporary limitations. These include the fact that students and staff, owing to the immense overgrowth of specialization, tend to be immersed in the routine of their immediate degree subjects. As a result, all wider issues are crowded out. Also, most universities in England are nonresidential and have little corporate life. Further, it is seen that only a small proportion of students have been brought up in homes where they are assured moral or religious convictions. St. Catharine's provides for students and staff to reside together for short periods of time, in order to examine the fundamental assumptions and implications of their own studies and also to explore the nature of man and society and the Christian interpretation of life in relation to the various secular alternatives.

St. Catharine's, while Christian, is definitely not propagandist.

Widely differing religious and political views are held by those who meet at Cumberland Lodge.

I was at St. Catharine's over a week end to sit in on a discussion of "The Motives of Science" by some twenty physicists who belonged to the Maxwell Society of the Physics Department of King's College, London. The Maxwell Society is one of a widely varying number of college groups that have come to Cumberland Lodge for weekend conferences. Approximately twenty postgraduate psychologists were also at the lodge for a program of discussion over this same weekend.

Questions that the physicists raised in the course of their discussion of "The Motives of Science" included the following: Has our drive to aid man only led him to greater danger? What do we mean by "responsibility"? What is the reason for helping one's neighbor? Can the motive of helping one's neighbor be justified within the language system of science, or can the answer be found only in the language systems of morality, philosophy and religion? Subtopics of the main theme included the following: (1) What have been the motives of scientists in the past? (2) The desire for power over the environment and our fellow-men, and also over our own expectations. (3) The desire for truth. (4) Prediction versus understanding. The itch to know "how" and "why," and in what sense this is a desire for truth. (5) The desire to help our fellow-men. This last issue was seen as involving the responsibilities of scientists to the community, in terms of medical research and scientific warfare.

It was obvious, at the summing-up session following the discussions, that the element of the scientist's responsibility was deeply disturbing to various individuals in the group. A final statement to attempt to answer the questions of responsibility in the language system of science was not conceivable if all the views represented were to be considered. Many answers to questions were advanced on a non-Christian, non-religious, nonmoral basis. Some final questions were themselves raised. These included: We have brought into existence things that give us the ability to control men's minds; where are they leading us? What are we going to do about something that happens, which we neither sought nor attempted to produce? When there are unforeseen results, what are the scientist's duties in regard to responsibilities growing out of that fact?

A number of books were cited as having a useful bearing on the topics discussed by the physicists in their attempt to deal with the subject, "The Motives of Science." These included: Bronowski, *The Common Sense of Science;* Burnham, *The Managerial Revolution;* Burtt, *Metaphysical Foundations of Modern Science;* Forster, *The Machine Breaks Down;* Oppenheimer, *Reith Lectures, 1953;* Orwell, *1984;* Whitehead, *Science and the Modern World.*

"Point of contact" in Christian communication is also sought by the Christian Frontier Council, comprising some forty men and women prominent in varied fields of activity. The Council asserts that men are called to glorify and obey God and to serve their neighbors in various spheres: international, national and local politics, industry, agriculture, commerce, finance, scientific research, the arts, culture, education, the family and the professions. The Council holds an evening meeting, about once a month, in London, and a specialist is often asked to be present to discuss his particular work. Each year an annual conference, over a long weekend, is held. Specialist groups have been formed to work intensively and continuously on specific projects. A quarterly publication, *Christian News-Letter,* is issued as the Council's organ. The publication of books under the Council's auspices is another function. *The Crisis in the University,* by Sir Walter Moberly, comes under this category; so does *The Doctor's Profession,* an inquiry into medical problems and the fruit of discussion by a Frontier group of doctors.

What is the Christian frontier?

By the frontier idea is meant recognition of the fact that there is this frontier between theology (in the sense of Christian dogma) and the multifarious spheres in which men have to act, or between the Church as an ecclesiastical institution and the tasks in which Christians have to obey God without direct ecclesiastical guidance. The perception that this frontier area exists and that it must be explored by fresh methods is sufficiently new to warrant the invention of this new name. . . . The Council does not seek to advertise itself, or to make claims which it is not in a position to fulfil. It may be described as an experiment in the possibilities of friendship, in which, through free intercourse, minds stimulate, quicken and enrich one another.[15]

One sphere of the Council's work is in the field of education. The Dons' Advisory Group is a Christian movement among university teachers in Great Britain and is supported jointly by the Christian Frontier Council and the Student Christian Movement. Michael B. Foster, an Oxford don and Council officer, wrote, in describing this activity: "Characteristic of the British movement is a fear of exclusiveness, of anything which might make the group of Christian Dons in a university a self-sufficient religious coterie. There is a dominating desire to keep the 'frontier' open, and to bring in colleagues who are on the fringe or beyond it."

In Scotland, in 1938, the Iona Community was established in order to find new ways of life and witness that would bridge the gap between industrial men and the Church. In the postwar world the Iona Community, under the leadership of George MacLeod and Ralph Morton, has found the task infinitely greater and more complex than originally conceived, because the world pattern, in which our social and industrial life is situated, has radically changed.

On the island of Iona, off the Scottish coast, a summer "laboratory" is conducted, in which visitors are invited to co-operate. Morning worship in the restored Abbey of Iona does not close with the Blessing. The evening service closes with the Blessing. In this way the day's work is seen as coming in between the first and second half of one complete act of worship. The purpose is that the work itself can become a means of glorifying God. Craftsmen at work on the Abbey are full fellow-members with ministers in the Iona Community, "making realistic discussion of how again, in the world, all work may become a vocation and a ministry." On the mainland, aside from the summer months on the island of Iona, the clergy members of the community translate into practice the various principles discussed and learned in the summer "laboratory" which includes lectures and discussions conducted by visiting Christian leaders. Many members work toward the building up of a strong community life in new housing sections, others seek to revitalize corporate Christian life in tired downtown parishes.

In France, the activity of the priest-workers (*prêtres-ouvriers*) and the pastor-workers has become one of the legendary and most controversial Christian "frontier" efforts of modern times. Pastor F. D. Fischer of France, lecturing in the 1955 Course for Theological Students at Bossey, Switzerland, spoke of Church people trying to proclaim the Gospel "over and across a wall." He described the "living and incarnational aspect" of Christianity in terms of some specific French experiments. "The only solution is for oneself to go on to the other side of the wall, to integrate oneself with the people one finds there." He told of a team of Protestant women called "The Team of the Outstretched

Hand." It comprises a deaconess, a midwife and a nurse. The team refuses to be paid, but instead evangelizes at its own expense. It seeks to live identically with the other persons in an extremely impoverished section of Paris. There is a whole participation in all the cultural forms of life there. Pastor Fischer said of a Roman Catholic priest-worker: "He confronts, in a valid theological way, Marxism with the Gospel." Pastor Fischer went on to say:

The press has projected a false light on the priest-workers and the pastor-workers. The work is not great adventure and heroism. It is simply an obedience to the Lord, sacrifice which is not of the day but every day. The disciple accepts to be crucified with his Lord, knowing that the Lord will show the power of His resurrection. The only power of communication is the Holy Spirit. When there is communication in Christ and following of Christ, then the Holy Spirit is present, the message is truly communicated.[16]

Among other attempts to find "point of contact" the *Kirchentag* movement in Germany should be mentioned, and *Wilgespruit* in South Africa, and a number of experiments in the United States such as Kirkridge, Parishfield, and other such centers.

Undoubtedly the most significant contemporary movement in Christian communication is the ecumenical movement. Christians from different church traditions, different lands and cultures, are brought together and enabled to pray together for the "wholeness" of Christ's Church to come on earth. There is no greater communications problem for Christians than the fact that Christians are divided one from another. There are many dangers resulting from this. One is that the divided churches cannot make a Christian witness in society strong enough to change the course of action of society. One may argue that the churches are more influenced by society than society is by the churches. The World Council of Churches is not *a* church, or *the* church, but is what its title says it is, a council of churches. Under its auspices, and within its fold, the churches make a common witness of service and study and mutual oblation.

A "typical" illustration of life at the Ecumenical Institute at the Chateau de Bossy, near Geneva in Switzerland, would be hard to find. Perhaps it would be the spontaneous gathering at a particular breakfast table in the dining room one morning while I was there, when I noted that our group (representing persons attending the annual Graduate School of the Ecumenical Institute) consisted of a missionary from the Belgian Congo; the Rev. Tien-Ho Chow of Fanling, Hong Kong; an Anglican candidate for Holy Orders from Cambridge University; a German theological student; the Rev. Aharon Sapsezian of São Paulo, Brazil, and myself. One does not seek to classify the "typical" at Bossey. The situation is fluid, the environment dynamic. Each person partaking of the experience of Bossey is forced, by the sheer impact of the ecumenical confrontation, to think more deeply in terms of his own confessional milieu and to rethink, fundamentally, his relationship in Christ with all other Christians.

The ecumenical movement is clearly not a watering-down process, a compromise in terms of sacrificing essential elements of faith, an idealistic attempt to arrive at a unity at any cost, or a pressurized steam-rolling process. It is realized that the unity of the Church will not be achieved by men in terms of wishful thinking or by their being moved emotionally. Nor will it be achieved by a few individuals who attempt to jump individually over fences, leaving their brethren behind. The individual's share in the corporate sin of division must be borne, not lightly set aside in a sentimental way. "Bless God for the hard lessons learned at Bossey, as well as for the more readily discernible riches." Thus Suzanne de Dietrich spoke in a retreat closing the 1954–55 Graduate School at Bossey.

The "hard lessons" were much in the minds of those listening to Miss de Dietrich. Those present had come really to grips with the sharp, deep divisions that separate Christians from Christians. The final note was not tinged in any way with sentiment or humanistic idealism. Yet the final note was, I feel strongly, a note of triumph and joy in the essential Oneness and Unity of the Church in Christ. This is, of course, a mystery in faith. This note was, in fact, intensified by the shared experience of grievous divisions, sin in corporate schism and the call to continual repentance before God.

Communication between Roman Catholics, who do not belong to the World Council of Churches, and non-Roman Catholics is fraught with tensions and difficulties. It was my privilege to spend two weeks in Paris at Istina, the Roman Catholic study center run by Dominicans. At Istina, a continuous study is made of ecumenical activities throughout the world and a major contribution is offered in ecumenical scholarship. A publication, *Istina,* is issued by Father Dumont and his associates.

We find in Roman Catholicism an ecumenical compulsion nourished by God the Holy Spirit. Leading spokesmen of this compulsion have included Father M. J. Congar; also Father George H. Tavard, who speaks of the vocation of the Roman Catholic ecumenist as being "to make the Church and the separated communions mutually understandable."[17] Father Congar states: "It is becoming no longer a question of confessional differences within Christendom itself, but of a radical choice between the Kingdom of God and the reign of Antichrist."[18] Roman Catholic ecumenism envisions "reunion" in terms of the "return" of non-Romans to the Roman Church.

The Greek Orthodox Church is strongly represented within the ecumenical movement. It was also my privilege to visit Constantinople (Istanbul) and to be received for luncheon and for a conversation by His Holiness, the Oecumenical Patriarch of Constantinople. Monsignor Athenagoras spoke to me of his intense concern for the unity of the world's Christians. Visiting at the Halki seminary, on the island of Heybeliada outside of Istanbul, and at the Apostoliki Diakonia in Athens, where I shared in the community life of some 200 Greek students, I could see the deep inroads being made by the ecumenical movement and some of the results of this. There is a renewed interest in increased theological preparation for priests, a desire to overcome the division between faith and life, and a sense of fellowship with other Christians. This must have a profound effect upon the Orthodox Church which, for centuries, had remained isolated from Western Christianity.

"Point of contact" is the recurring theme running through the work of the sharply varying Christian "frontier" activities that we have briefly examined. Paul Tillich has made this observation:

We can speak to people only if we participate in their concern—not by condescension, but by sharing in it. We can point to the Christian answer only if, on the other hand, we are not identical with them. And thirdly, we can use these people and their ideas to awaken those among our group who are still living in a secure tower. We can awaken them to the elements in themselves which are usually covered by an assumed knowledge of all answers.[19]

We perceive, in these diverse projects in Christian communication, a Christian reaching-out to men and women who are encased in the rigid institutional moulds and arbitrary classifications of modern life. This reaching-out is honest and intelligent: it involves the Christian in new thought and action patterns. The reaching-out becomes participation, a sharing in concern. And there is a by-product of this zealous and Spirit-filled activity. The Gospel message is clarified, for communicator as well as for the person receiving communication. Crustations that had been added to the essential Gospel message are hewn away. The crisis and demand of the kerygma stand out in stark relief for persons who have long felt the Christian Gospel could not possibly be related to *this* kind of work or to *that* sort of life. Christ is proclaimed Lord of all life; and this is seen to be immediately relevant in a telling way for men and women who are caught up in life but who have forgotten that Christianity is a living faith for the living.

POINT OF CONTACT IN EVANGELIZING INSTITUTIONS

Discovering "point of contact" is a basic requirement in a major task awaiting the Church in its evangelizing mission: the penetration of the institutions which encase the mass media. Men are involved in institutions, as members of institutions. Men are moulded by institutions. It is our task to penetrate these, to speak to these by establishing relation with them. How is the Church to penetrate the institutions that comprise the media of mass communication—for example, a great metropolitan newspaper organization, a broadcasting network, a film studio or a film distribution organization, or the integrated organism that is a mass-circulation magazine?

Persons make up the institutions mentioned above. The Church exists to carry on the work of Christ in the world today. Christ, the Son of God, Who became man for us men and for our salvation, is a Person. Persons, men and women, carry on Christ's work in His Church under the guidance of God the Holy Spirit.

Persons represent each institution—the Church and, say, the newspaper—in any relation between the two. A clergyman meets a city editor, a Woman's Auxiliary member knows a church editor, a vestryman lives next door to a rewrite man, and so on. The clergy and the laymen and laywomen of the Church, accepting their responsibility and tasks as members of the Body of Christ, realize that Christian education is a part of each Christian's duty. What is so misunderstood and unknown today as Christianity? Where can Christian education better be carried on than in the byways of the world, in the market places and, let us say, in the newspaper offices (or film, broadcasting or telecasting studios), in the homes of future newspapermen, in the schools where future newspapermen are being educated? What is more vital for Christian Education than to make the Church relevant to the average person in his everyday life, work, play, decisions, motives?

How are we to penetrate an institution such as a major studio of the motion picture industry or a network operation of the television industry or a newspaper plant? There is no blueprint available for such a long-range project. And there can never be a blueprint for such a work, because it is a work of God the Holy Spirit. There will always be differences in circumstances, human factors and "point of contact." But there are certain basic, discernible facts.

Ideally, a clergyman or a team of clergy and laymen and laywomen, would set out upon such a project in terms of at least a "ten year plan." And, despite many temptations, the task at hand would always be to establish relation, and never to exploit. For the clergyman or individual clergy members of a team, it would be absolutely essential to recognize that *he is in a parish* while engaged in such work. At the same time that another clergyman is paying a more traditional type of parish call within a home near to his church building, a clergyman involved in this institutional-missionary endeavor might be paying a parish call, too—but within a TV studio. At the same time that another clergyman is sitting in a parish office (a traditional type of parish office, located within his church building or near it), a mass media missioner might be sitting in *his* parish office—and it could be a projection room, or a room in a downtown office building.

It is necessary for a clergyman working in such a complex and creative field as mass media of communication to recognize the world of difference between guidance and liaison, on the one hand, and intrusion and creative conflict, on the other. Being a missioner in mass media might involve a cleric in a liaison function between Church and industry in terms of working on a particular religious radio or TV program. Quite without becoming aware of it, the clergyman might become a counterpart of the dreaded "sponsor's wife." She became infamous in advertising circles, radio and TV, as the symbol of unnecessary tampering with creative efforts, with authority that had to be handled with kid gloves, while regarded with fear and contempt for having "no talent." An honest definition of the task at hand, coupled with a Christian concept of human dignity and creative freedom, will reveal the scope of an individual's operations.

In establishing relation with industry, as a mass media missioner, a clergyman would want to become acquainted with as many persons as possible, and at all levels, from executive hierarchy to the youngest and newest employee. Might it not eventually be possible that clergy would be called upon to assist in the training program of employees and in specialized training and refresher programs for executives? In England, industry is beginning to find it needs and wants such service. This is a change from the atmosphere of suspicion formerly found. Some years ago Archbishop Temple recounted the following incident:

When a group of Bishops attempted to bring Government, Coal-Owners and Miners together in a solution of the disastrous Coal Strike of 1926, Mr. Baldwin, then Prime Minister, asked how the Bishops would like it if he referred to the Iron and Steel Federation the revision of the Athanasian Creed, and this was acclaimed as a legitimate score.[20]

Recently, it was pointed out that the Sheffield Industrial Mission makes a regular contribution in all interworks conferences for managers and foremen at the invitation of the area training department—of the British Iron and Steel Federation.

Suppose that a missioner in mass media found such a channel, what would he discuss with his parishioners?

He would take a leaf from the book of the industrial missioner. He would deal with Christian principles that need to be translated into quite technical industrial and professional terms. He would discuss justice and would attempt to translate it into the terms of the sound stage, the office, the agency business. He would discuss love in terms of brotherhood among men and would attempt to deal with this on the level of everyday relationships, of tensions, of exploitation and conflict, of the goal of an individual working in the mass media. He would discuss a feeling of responsibilty on the part of a mass media worker toward the institution for which he works and toward his co-workers. Is he using the institution simply as a steppingstone to another institution, or is he content to spiral upwards within the one institution, or is he as interested in the institution as in his own career, or is a combination of these factors ascertainable in his particular case? Is he using his co-workers as living stepping-stones to higher position and greater power, is he manipulating them, or, on the other hand, is he totally indifferent to them? The missioner would discuss Work itself, attempting to instill in his hearers an esteem and a high understanding of it. Is it a means, always, to an end—or is it an end in itself, a part of the natural process of life, an activity of the very Godhead?

As a mass media missioner, one might be called upon, as mentioned above, to assist in a particular radio and TV program, or film, or publications development. If so involved, one ought not to "hit and run," but to take time to learn about the industry. One should strive sincerely to care for the industry. Redeeming a mass medium of communication for Christ does not mean having "religious" programs on the air twenty-four hours a day! It does mean converted persons. It does mean, in time, an industry attitude that is Christian in the sense of loving rather than exploiting; and this in terms of Christian relationships in work, Christian goals, Christians expressing their baptismal status, *here,* in the communications industry.

Another means of penetrating a mass medium of communication is that of Christian scholarship. Books, specific studies, research projects need to be undertaken. But these would be read not for any falsely pietistic reasons, but because they are essential and good and practical. And here we reach an important point in our thinking. Such work would be the natural result of caring for the industry; of performing Christ's work of caring for the industry; of serving the Kingdom of God with one's mind; of wanting the industrial institution to measure up to its very best, as Christ wants that. Surely the Christian, performing Christ's work in the world, will care as much for the industrial institution as anyone else cares for it. Surely the Christian, redeeming for Christ and enabled by Christ, will love the medium of mass communication more than someone who is simply exploiting the mass medium! And this love will express itself in a number of ways, including Christian scholarship, for the benefit of the institution.

It is vital that the work of a missioner in mass media be correlated with parish life. There are manifold problems in the incorporation of professional and industrial persons, newly converted, into traditional parish life. For "old" and "new" Christians to mix has always taxed the charity of each. All the psychological strain of acceptance and self-acceptance, all the elements of status, all the difficulties of "different languages," enter into the problem. Often, in the past, there has occurred at this stage a breakdown in the total process of evangelization of the "new" Christians. Sometimes the seeds of tragedy have been sown by an unnatural "great effort" to assimilate and to go along. But the problem could be overcome if everyone were natural, and if everyone involved would *openly* and *together* face the very real problem. In fact, the existence of the problem provides an unusually good opportunity for everyone to move together to the foot of the Cross. There is no better position for the reception of God's grace.

I should like to make a suggestion in regard to this integration into parish life of individuals involved in such a process of institutional evangelization. In New York or Hollywood, for example, the individual persons in a communications institution (a movie studio, a TV network, a magazine) who had become assimilated into the work of the mass media mission would be members of widely scattered church congregations. In the case of New York, some might be members of a church in White Plains, some in Greenwich, some in New Jersey; in the case of Hollywood, some might be members of a church in Encino, some in Bel Air, some in Pacific Palisades, or Pasadena or Studio City. These individuals would be divided up into many parishes. Yet there would be a need for a singleness of corporate purpose grounded in corporate worship. There would be a need for a corporate parish consciousness within industry. There would also be a need for the laity and clergy to come together once a week, at a lunch or evening meeting, to discuss their work and to undergo a continuing and related instruction pertaining to that work. An evening might be the better time for this, while lunch-time activity would be the finest opportunity for individual evangelism. One would not want to tie up too many lunch periods for "Church work" when they could be employed for Church work. This reminds me of the reply that a baker gave when asked what Church work he did. He answered, "I bake." A Christian is a Christian, and serves as a Christian, where he lives and works as a Christian.

A "Christian withdrawal" into "Christian" publications (or other mass media of communication), out of the market place, out of the front lines of war against that which is un-Christian—such a thing contradicts what it means to be Christian. The Christian, in Holy Baptism, is received into the congregation of Christ's flock, "manfully to fight under His banner" and "to continue Christ's faithful soldier and servant unto his life's end." There are things to fight against as a faithful soldier; there are jobs to be done as a servant of the Kingdom of God.

In the British film, *Lease of Life,* a country vicar is catapulted into sudden fame and is approached by the representative of a big London newspaper with an offer to write some articles. When the vicar cannot seem to make up his mind about the matter, the newspaperman tells him: "Dean Inge was a pillar of the Church, but he was also two columns in the *Evening Standard."* Did the movie-makers understand the deep significance of this little speech? I think not, because the vicar's face registered strained surprise and distaste about the whole thing. The value of a newspaper column by the late Dean, by the vicar in the film or by any Christian surely is not to be measured in terms of "evangelistic technique" or of "a cheap publicity stunt." The basic fact is that the newspaper is God's; as a part of His kingdom and creation, it is to be claimed and reclaimed for Him.

We need to pray, not only for parishioners, but for such things as newspapers and radio networks and film operations. If a newspaper is sick, pray that God's will may be accomplished in it; that it may be made healthy and whole. If a newspaper is healthy, thank God for it. Offer prayers for newspapers in church. Have, in church, a particular Sunday when the men and women who work in the field of communications are gathered in. Offer thanks to God for them, pray for their continual enabling and strengthening by Him.

The trouble lies surely with the Church if "church people" are seen as standing over on one side, away from men and women like "newspaper people." Of course, "newspaper people" are then forced to react by laughing up their sleeves at "church people." It is high time that we took more seriously the *wholeness* of God's world, including media of mass communication such as newspapers; and that we applied to this wholeness of the world the scriptural text: "God was in Christ reconciling the world unto Himself." The men and women who are members of the Church are called out of the world, and then sent back into it again. The *redeemed* Fellowship goes out on the job of *redeeming* the world for Christ.

Yes, the Body of Christ has work to do. This is that *kind* of work. It is always a judgment upon us as Christians when any newspaperman or TV producer or any other man in the world can quite sincerely ask: "Is the Church interested in *us*—in *me?"* The Church, interested in the salvation of each person simply by reason of being the Church, needs increasingly to reach *persons* encased within *institutions.* The "brave new world" has been marked by the tendency to classify persons in groups, strata, departments, institutions. The Church has to find persons where they are, in such contexts, and then to restore to such persons the dignity of individual personality in the sight of God.

"PERSONAL" MASS COMMUNICATION

Point of Contact. These three words are often employed quite naively yet, when we deal with them, we find that we are plunged into a crucial doctrinal examination of revelation. Needless to say, "evangelism" undergoes re-evaluation in light of such examination. "Point of contact" has been treated, in a theological way, by three eminent theologians, Karl Barth, Emil Brunner and Paul Tillich. Karl Barth insists that the Holy Spirit stands in need of no "point of contact" but that which He creates.[21] Barth's contempt for an obvious "point of contact," indeed for a vulgarization of it, fills a great need. Yet it seems that Barth might err in the delicate tension between useful criticism and a rigid, absolute position.

Tillich deals with "point of contact" (*anknüpfungspunkt*) in his "method of correlation." Tillich poses the quesiton: Can the Christian message be adapted to the modern mind without losing its essential and unique character? He tries to correlate question and answer, situation and message, human existence and divine manifestation.[22] For Tillich, God in His self-manifestation to man is dependent on the way man receives this manifestation. Man must ask the deep questions to which revelation gives the answers. Indeed, there is no revelation if there is no one who receives it as his ultimate concern; revelation is always an event subjective and objective in strict interdependence. Tillich asserts the necessity of a history of revelation for a final revelation, by way of preparation for it.

Emil Brunner, having become entangled in the concepts of "form" and "matter," asserts a burning interest in making the Word "intelligible," yet his concern seems somehow sadly weakened in view of his accepting man's literal inability to receive the Word. Of course, Brunner maintains that, even as a sinner, as the "natural man," man is never without revelation. Sin can only be understood as an "active-actual-negation" of this revelation. Revelation, for Brunner, is not something that is added to man's being; it is there even when it is denied, rejected and ignored. Man is seen as being different from the rest of creation because, through the original revelation in creation, he is a responsible being. Even as one who denies God, the rational man is a proof of the existence of God; he could not deny God had he not an original knowledge of Him. Here, Brunner comes to the very crux of "point of contact." True faith begins, he says, when a person no longer hides from himself the fact of his distress; when he has no further illusions about it, nor about the fact that this need is great and that it is of a specific kind. Brunner claims that the Christian faith cannot strike root save in the heart of a person who *recognizes* that his need is desperate. A man perceives that his need is desperate only when he sees that it is not outside himself at all but deeply imbedded within his very self.[23]

Barth is little concerned with technical "communication."[24] Herein he seems to be weak. For surely the question is not simply that we live in a world and an era of technical, mass culture and have a certain choice as to how much we shall ourselves employ specific media, but rather that we are ourselves being evangelized far more than we are even considering evangelizing others.

Man is seen by some as a digit, a point in a computed rating, a sales statistic, a reaction, a subject of psychological depth research, a potential buyer at the box office, a TV viewer, a radio listener, a newspaper or magazine reader. Thus there is a secular "point of contact"; there is a demonic "point of contact," which seeks man to exploit him. But we must find a "point of contact" for *praeparatio evangelica,* which may be a correlating of "negative witness" to the revelation which completes it, as well as being explicit positive witness. Tillich is on solid ground as regards this latter "point of contact" approach.

Tillich's thinking is clearly expressed in various of his writings. He says that man has become aware that man himself is the door to the deeper levels of reality, that man in his own existence has the only possible approach to existence itself. And this fact is why many persons are moved by a "religious" motivation to go to the theatre rather than to the church. For such persons, there is no longer a "point of contact" in words and symbols, and reality seems to have been sucked out of the church situation, leaving only a dry shell.

But, in the theatre (or, surely, the novel, the TV drama, the film, the newspaper) there is vicarious identification with reality. Yet Jesus Christ is reality. How has the Church managed in so many places, at so many times, seemingly to rob its Lord of His reality? As Tillich points out, such churches have lapsed back into preparation themselves, have lost any dynamic correlation with the realities of life.

A theonomous society will be marked by aesthetic reason's neither being subject to ecclesiastical or political prescripts nor producing secular art cut off from the depth of aesthetic reason; "through its autonomous artistic forms, it points to the New Being which has appeared in final revelation."[25] The artist (as the "saint"; or, the artist becoming "saintly") becomes "transparent." Christian communication must be earmarked by being "transparent." Only if this is the case is "point of contact" valid. When this is the case, then God indeed works through instruments of which He is sovereign; and, aided by men with their free wills who have by His grace become to a degree "transparent," "point of contact" is achieved in time and society. Tillich's "method of correlation" seems preferable to Barthian absolutism. If we move too far afield to exalt Holiness, we end up with the stunning conclusion that our "god is too small"; and that, in asserting an attribute of "otherness," we have seemingly succeeded in relegating God out of His omnipotence and omnipresence.

In this way, Tillichian "correlation" may be applied to the media of mass communication. In our evangelism within media of mass communication, we are sure to be aware of two different approaches: the explicitly Christian medium of communication and the implicitly Christian medium. Many media today claiming to be "religious" or even "Christian" are neither religious nor Christian; our contemporary religious enthusiasm in the United States makes religion pay off in dollars and cents in terms of various media. The majority of Hollywood films with "religious" themes are merely exploiting this enthusiasm to add dollars to the box office "take" by adding God to the star roster. Many quite "sincere" TV and radio programs, labeled as "religious" or "Christian," are merely sentimental. Yet within the area of various media that have no expressed idea of being religious or interest in being Christian, we find the deep questions concerning the human situation coming to the surface. Many a very bad movie is, at least, dealing at a particular level with man's existential condition.

A major task for the churches is to perceive clearly this "negative witness" in so much of contemporary expression, and to point the way to converting that very "negative witness" into a "positive Christian witness." The theatre has often become far more effective today than the pulpit in expressing man's realistic condition, in voicing questions that man asks within his own soul. The pulpit needs to thank the theatre for such honest and effective expression of man's *questions;* and then the pulpit needs to convey to man the *answer* of God's revelation of Himself in Christ. Often it is impossible to present Christian proclamation explicitly unless there has first been a *praeparatio evangelica* by means of implicit Christian witness. The multifaceted implicit witness in "negative witness," in our technical society, needs to be redeemed in the sense of being correlated and fulfilled in explicit witness.

One of the most vivid statements of a man's desperate search for the "point of contact" with other men is that given us by Henri Perrin, a Roman Catholic priest, who voluntarily joined other Frenchmen who had been conscripted by the occupying Germans for slave labor in Nazi munition factories during the Second World War. Father Perrin was imprisoned with men who did not know Christ, who were absolutely indifferent to Christ. I know of few comparable documents on the subject of the crisis of Christian communication. Father Perrin reached some definite conclusions:

> *All this calls for men who can get out of themselves, who will cease walking by lonely paths, and will come to the high roads where men of all nations pass by. Such Christians are these, leaping over the rottenness of the world at a bound, will stand up before men, bearing the light of Christ past the winding ways and false mysticisms which mislead them. This also calls for men to leave the Ghetto in which they so often shut themselves up—in* our *churches,* our *papers,* our *movements,* our *good works. . . . This calls for them to be amongst pagans, and really become theirs as Christ became ours, giving up their life, their time, their resources, their activity, for those who haven't yet heard the "good tidings." A Christian hasn't finished his job when he has gone to Mass on Sunday. The Church's prayer, and the body of Christ, are only given him as a help towards bringing HIM to the world. And if men do not recognize in us the love and goodness of our Father, then we have done* nothing*—we haven't even begun to serve Him.*[26]

Our ordinary encounters with other human beings lack the kind of drama one finds in, for example, Father Perrin's exciting account of his ordeal within Nazi prisons. Yet we ride on subways and buses, we walk along streets, we sit at drugstore and luncheon counters, we sit in crowded theatres in ink-black solitariness—*alongside persons.* Who are they? Can we possibly hope to determine, behind an empty smile, the degree in another human being of loneliness, spiritual fatigue, fear, rejection or despair? At our physical "point of contact," anonymity at the elbow of anonymity, is any communication established? Is it a demonic communication of exploitation and overlapping monologues, or is it Christian communication between "persons" who recognize their kinship in Christ?

We cannot approach the media of mass communication, TV, the press, the film, radio, as if physical communication did not exist. Of course, physical communication may be "individual" but not "personal," and so it becomes demonic. Even sexual union may represent, not "personal" communication, but merely impersonal contact, crude exploitation and a severe, strange heightening of essential isolation. Inversely, mass communication, while not being "individual," may seem to be "personal" in a most compelling way. This it does by speaking to the universal human situation of finitude and estrangement. How does a personality, using a mass medium, sometimes achieve so intense a communications impact upon an individual in the mass that the impact seems to be greater than that achieved by personal communication? The answer lies partially in the factor of *empathy.* Webster defines it as "imaginative projection of one's own consciousness into another being." An American radio executive has described it in this way: "You know, the ability to get inside other people, to understand exactly how they're feeling." Arthur Godfrey, whose success as a dominant personality in American life is explained by others in terms of empathy, explains it himself in this way: "It's because people believe in me. How the hell else can you explain it?"[27] Mr. Godfrey's approach to the mass media is rather remarkable, and has had a remarkable effect in determining how the mass media are used. It had been during a long hospitalization, following an automobile accident, that Godfrey determined how best he could communicate to that audience that would exist only when he caused it to come together by his communication, by his empathy.

Godfrey spent hours listening to the radio. "Those days we were all talking to the ladies and gentlemen of the radio audience. *I decided there wasn't any such audience. There was just one guy or one girl off somewhere listening by themselves. Hell, if they were together, they'd have something better to do than listen to the radio.*"[28]

There are women in America who feel that they share in a more meaningful relationship of personal communication with Godfrey than they do with their husbands. The same could be said in regard to several other dominant personalities in American life who have made an incredibly deep impression upon society by use of the media of mass communication. Mass communication, while not being "individual" communication, frequently bears some of the earmarks of "personal" communication in a way whose power we have not even begun to probe.

I know a well-educated, middle-aged woman, an Anglican and for many years a faithful and steady participant in the sacramental life, who has recently started listening to the regular broadcast sermons of the Rev. Ralph W. Sockman. The words of Dr. Sockman are now quite as important to her spiritual life and well-being, she maintains, as is her regular participation in the Holy Eucharist. From the standpoint of the woman's background, this is a situation calling for a careful analysis, which could yield surprising conclusions.

It must be said that the factor that seemingly makes mass communication "personal" is not necessarily also making it Christian. An illusory "personal" type of mass communication may well be demonic communication in which empathy is used to manipulate people. In the media of mass communication there is the identical communication problem one finds in human encounters at the theatre, on the bus, at the luncheon counter or on the street. Human problems of anxiety, fear, rejection and loneliness remain the same, whether a person is sitting at home in front of a TV set or standing in a crowded subway. The solution, in either case, lies in personal communication, in relatedness, in the "meeting" of "persons." However, an illusory or simulated kind of "personal" communication may be as dangerous as real personal communication is healing. Such illusory "personal" communication may be merely an egocentric expression of exploitation that obscures, rather than magnifies, the Lord, substituting the glamour of the celebrity for the glory of God. There is a mysterious power limitation upon such illusory "personal" communication. Though it may lead one into a collectivism in which one's existence as a "person" is threatened, it cannot lead one into real "community" in which one freely seeks relationship as a person with other persons.

It is ironical that mass communication, while it exerts a tremendous influence upon individuals, yet can never achieve the kind or degree of impact that is the result of personal communication representing a relationship of persons. Mass communication may indeed move an individual, but it may not establish a personal relationship (despite all the exploited empathy up anybody's sleeve). A community of related persons is a vastly different thing from an audience of several thousand individuals watching one man on TV, or listening to him over the radio. The several thousand individuals may be relating to several thousand different images of the one personality.

In the Age of Publicity, is our sense of the "numinous" becoming reserved, in a startling and scarcely understood way, for the celebrity, the hem of whose garment it is thrilling to touch even if it is not a healing action? God demands a response, but so does the exploitation expert. It sometimes seems deceptively simpler to be a member of a computed mass and to buy, on schedule, so many boxes of cold cereal, and a deodorant, and even an easy book about an easy god, than to be a person and to make the revolutionary, the personal response to the demand of Christ—and, so, to be torn asunder, and to throw away one's "security" in return for mere "faith."

FOOTNOTES FOR POINT OF CONTACT

[1] Hendrik Kraemer, "The Problem of Communication," Laidlaw Lectures, Knox Theological Seminary, Toronto, Jan., 1956.
[2] Sydney Cave, *The Christian Way,* p. 24.
[3] Jean Danielou, *Advent,* p. 8.
[4] T. S. Eliot, *The Cocktail Party,* p. 188.
[5] Brother George Every, *op. cit.,* p. 58.
[6] Dorothy L. Sayers, *op. cit.,* p. 19.
[7] Thomas Whiteside, *op. cit.,* p. 40.
[8] Reinhold Niebuhr, *Beyond Tragedy,* p. 28.
[9] Malcolm Boyd, "House-Church: Visual Aid," *Episcopal Churchnews,* p. 28, Feb. 6, 1955.
[10] Malcolm Boyd, "The Industrial Mission," *Episcopal Churchnews,* p. 27, March 6, 1955.
[11] Malcolm Boyd, "Comics With A Goal," *Episcopal Churchnews,* p. 16, Dec. 11, 1955.
[12] *Ibid.*
[13] *An Experimental Centre,* pp. 11–12.
[14] Malcolm Boyd, "New Ways To Communicate," *The Christian Century,* p. 271, Feb. 29, 1956.
[15] "The Christian Frontier," *The Frontier,* pp. 32–38, Jan., 1950.

[16] Malcolm Boyd, "Christians On The Assembly Line," *Episcopal Churchnews,* p. 26, Sept. 4, 1955.
[17] George H. Tavard, *The Catholic Approach to Protestantism,* p. 154.
[18] M. J. Congar, O. P., *Divided Christendom.* (A Catholic Study of the Problem of Reunion). Trans. M. A. Bousfield, p. 275.
[19] Paul Tillich, "Communicating the Gospel," *Union Seminary Quarterly Review,* p. 7, June, 1952.
[20] William Temple, *Christianity and Social Order,* p. 9.
[21] Karl Barth's reply to Emil Brunner, "Nein!," *Natural Theology,* pp. 144ff. See also: Barth, *The Doctrine of the Word of God,* p. 283.
[22] Paul Tillich, *Systematic Theology, Vol. I,* p. 8.
[23] Emil Brunner, *Revelation and Reason,* p. 423.
[24] Karl Barth, "Nein!," *op. cit.,* p. 127.
[25] Paul Tillich, *Systematic Theology, op. cit.,* p. 149.
[26] Henri Perrin, *Priest-Workman in Germany,* pp. 227–8.
[27] "Oceans of Empathy," *Time,* p. 75, Feb. 27, 1950.
[28] *Ibid.*

A LITANY FOR CHRISTIAN COMMUNICATION

O God the Father, Who at sundry times and in divers manners hast spoken in time past unto the fathers by the prophets, and who hast spoken unto us by thy Son;

Have mercy upon us.

O God the Son, the Word of God, Thou who wast made flesh and didst dwell among us, and Whose glory we beheld, the glory as of the only begotten of the Father;

Have mercy upon us.

O God the Holy Spirit, Who filled the Apostles on the day of Pentecost so that they began to speak with other tongues as Thou didst give them utterance, and so that the multitude heard them speak in many tongues the wonderful works of God;

Have mercy upon us.

Remember not the words of worship we have prayed to false gods and have uttered unto Thee with our lips but not with our heart's consent; remember not the words of hatred and malice we have spoken to our neighbor, nor our withholding of words of understanding and love from him;

Spare us, good Lord.

From changing communication into exploitation; from much speaking but little listening; from speaking to our neighbor in monologue rather than in dialogue; from utter isolation and the end of communication;

Good Lord, deliver us.

We beseech Thee to hear us that Thou wilt enable us to speak Thy Word, intelligibly and in integrity and by all the means that Thou hast given us, to persons whom we encounter in all the market places and on all the frontiers of life;

We beseech Thee to hear us, good Lord.

That Thou, who art love, wilt enable us to be Thine instruments so that we may obey Thy command to communicate Thy Word to all the world;

We beseech Thee to hear us, good Lord.

That Thou wilt turn us from our accusations and counteraccusations, our rationalizations and our lack of repentance, enabling us to penetrate with Thy Word the barriers of our self-interest and self-assertion;

We beseech Thee to hear us, good Lord.

That Thou wilt guide us out of the Christian ghetto into the main stream and into the front lines of life, and enable our tongues to proclaim there the scandal of Thy Gospel;

We beseech Thee to hear us, good Lord.

That Thou wilt show us the human loneliness and rejection hidden by the empty smile and, in our human encounters of anonymity at the elbow of anonymity enable us to enter into relationship with other persons as subjects to love and not as objects to use, surrendering our flag of self-interest and our sword of resentment;

We beseech Thee to hear us, good Lord.

That Thou wilt look with pity upon us who are closer together than ever before in our technologically induced togetherness, yet are farther apart from one another in charity, compassion, a sense of mutual responsibility and an understanding of one another's efforts at communication;

We beseech Thee to hear us, good Lord.

That Thou wilt gird us for the battle we must do against indifference, speaking through our actions and lives when issues are no longer intelligibly discussed and words have lost their meaning; giving us light to penetrate our prejudices and delusions;

We beseech Thee to hear us, good Lord.

That Thou wilt edify our thinking which has been penetrated by pagan symbols of success, and clear the blurred focus with which we look at the Cross;

We beseech Thee to hear us, good Lord.

That Thou wilt guide us in our Christian use of the media of mass communication so that we claim them only for Thee, O Lord, because they are Thine; guide us so that we may not be guilty of the blasphemy of exploitation of these media in Thy Name and in the name of Thy Church;

We beseech Thee to hear us, good Lord.

That we may be enabled to find Thy Word in all words, to proclaim the Christian truth which is present in all creative work;

We beseech Thee to hear us, good Lord.

That we may proclaim the Gospel story of the Manger and the Cross, of the Resurrection, the Ascension and Pentecost;

We beseech Thee to hear us, good Lord.

That Thou wilt use us in Thy speaking to all men and each man, that our communication may be sacramental in proclaiming vocation, pronouncing Thy Truth, changing the course of lives and events; that we may communicate Christian tension in the midst of un-Christian peace, and communicate that peace which passeth all understanding in the midst of the Christian's war;

We beseech Thee to hear us, good Lord.

O Lord, arise, help us, and deliver us for Thine honour.

O God, be Thou our love; O Christ, be Thou our Word; O Holy Spirit, be Thou our power.

Glory be to the Father, and to the Son, and to the Holy Ghost,

As it was in the beginning, is now, and ever shall be, world without end. Amen.

BIBLIOGRAPHY

BOOKS, PAMPHLETS AND UNPUBLISHED PAPERS

AN EXPERIMENTAL CENTRE. (The First Decade: 1943–1953). London: St. Anne's House, 1953.

BARTH, KARL. *The Doctrine of the Word of God*. Trans. G. T. Thomson. New York: Charles Scribner's Sons, 1936.

———. *The Epistle to the Romans*. Trans. (from the Sixth Edition) Edwyn C. Hoskyns. London: Oxford University Press, 1937.

BARTON, ROGER. *Advertising Agency Operations and Management*. New York: McGraw-Hill Book Company, Inc., 1955.

BENNETT, JOHN C. *Christian Ethics and Social Policy*. New York: Charles Scribner's Sons, 1953.

BERDYAEV, NICHOLAS. *The Fate of Man in the Modern World*. Trans. Donald A. Lowrie. New York: Morehouse Publishing Company, 1935.

BONHOEFFER, DIETRICH. *Letters and Papers from Prison*. Trans. Reginald H. Fuller. London. SCM Press, Ltd., 1953.

BROOKS, JOHN NIXON, JR. *The Big Wheel*. New York: Harper & Brothers, 1949.

BRUNNER, HEINRICH EMIL. *Revelation and Reason*. Trans. Olive Wyon. Philadelphia: The Westminster Press, 1946.

BRUNNER, HEINRICH EMIL AND BARTH, KARL. *Natural Theology* (Comprising "Nature and Grace" by Dr. Brunner and the reply "No!" by Dr. Barth).

Trans. Peter Fraenkel. Introduction by John Baillie. London: Geoffrey Bles, The Centenary Press, 1946.

BUBER, MARTIN. *I and Thou.* Trans. Ronald Gregor Smith. Edinburgh: T. & T. Clark, 1937.

BUSCH, NOEL F. *Briton Hadden: A Biography of the Co-Founder of Time.* New York: Farrar, Straus and Cudahy, Inc., 1949.

CASSERLEY, J. V. LANGMEAD. *The Retreat From Christianity In The Modern World.* New York: Longmans, Green & Company, 1952.

CAVE, SYDNEY. *The Christian Way.* New York: The Philosophical Library, 1951.

COLQUHOUN, FRANK. *Harringay Story.* (A detailed account of The Greater London Crusade, 1954). London: Hodder and Stoughton, 1955.

CONGAR, M. J., O. P. *Divided Christendom.* Trans. M. A. Bousfield. London: Geoffrey Bles, The Centenary Press, 1939.

DANIELOU, JEAN. *Advent.* Trans. Rosemary Sheed. New York: Sheed & Ward, 1951.

DEMANT, VIGO AUGUSTE. *Christian Polity.* London: Faber & Faber Limited, 1936.

DENCH, ERNEST A. *Making the Movies.* New York: The Macmillan Company, 1915.

ELIOT, T. S. *The Cocktail Party.* New York: Harcourt, Brace & Company, 1950.

———. *The Idea of a Christian Society.* London: Faber & Faber Limited, 1939.

Evangelism—The Mission of the Church to Those Outside Her Life. (An Ecumenical Survey prepared under the auspices of the World Council of Churches). London: SCM Press, Ltd., 1954.

Evangelism in France (Quarry Article). Geneva: World Council of Churches, Secretariat for Evangelism, 1952.

Evangelism in Holland (Quarry Article). Geneva: World Council of Churches, Secretariat for Evangelism, 1950.

Evangelism in Scotland (Quarry Article). Geneva: World Council of Churches, Secretariat for Evangelism, 1954.

Evanston Speaks (Reports from the Second Assembly of the World Council of Churches). London: SCM Press Ltd., 1954.

EVERY, BROTHER GEORGE. *Christian Discrimination.* London: The Sheldon Press, 1940.

FITZGERALD, F. SCOTT. *The Last Tycoon.* New York: Charles Scribner's Sons, 1941.

FORSYTH, P. T. *The Work of Christ.* London: Independent Press, Ltd., 1952.

FROMM, ERICH. *The Sane Society.* New York: Rinehart & Company, Inc., 1955.

HOCKING, WILLIAM ERNEST. *Freedom of the Press.* Chicago: University of Chicago Press, 1947.

HODGES, H. A. *Christianity and the Modern World View.* London: SCM Press Ltd., 1949.

HOUSE, FRANCIS H. "Religious Broadcasting." *A Christian Year Book.* London: SCM Press Ltd., 1950. Pp. 133 ff.

HUTCHISON, JOHN ALEXANDER (ed.) *Christian Faith and Social Action.* New York: Charles Scribner's Sons, 1953.

ISHERWOOD, CHRISTOPHER. *Prater Violet.* New York: Random House, 1945.

KATZ, ELIHU AND LAZARSFELD, PAUL F. *Personal Influence: The Part Played by People in the Flow of Mass Communications.* Glencoe, Illinois: The Free Press, 1955.

KIERKEGAARD, SOREN. *For Self-Examination.* Trans. Walter Lowrie. Princeton University Press, 1944.

———. *Fear and Trembling* and *The Sickness Unto Death.* Trans. Walter Lowrie. Garden City: Doubleday & Company, Inc., 1954.

KRAEMER, HENDRIK. "The Problem of Communication." Laidlaw Lectures, Knox Theological Seminary, Toronto, January, 1956.

KRONENBERGER, LOUIS. *Company Manners.* Indianapolis: The Bobbs-Merrill Company, Inc., 1954.

LEWIS, C. S. "Hamlet: The Prince or The Poem?" (Annual Shakespeare Lecture of the British Academy). *From the Proceedings of the British Academy.* London: Humphrey Milford, 1942.

MACLEOD, GEORGE. *We Shall Re-Build.* Philadelphia: Kirkbridge, 1954.

MCLUHAN, MARSHALL. "Educational Effects of the Mass Media of Communication." Paper presented at one of the inaugural discussion groups on the occasion of the inauguaration of Hollis L. Caswell as President of Teachers College, Columbia University, November 21, 1955.

MCMAHAN, HARRY WAYNE. *The Television Commercial.* New York: Hastings House, Publishers, Inc., 1954.

MICHONNEAU, ABBE G. *Revolution in a City Parish.* Westminster, Maryland: The Newman Press, 1949.

———. *The Missionary Spirit in Parish Life.* Westminster, Maryland: The Newman Press, 1952.

MILES, DR. VIRGINIA. "What Makes People Do Things?". Address delivered before the Grocery Manufacturers of America, at the Greenbriar, June 21, 1955.

MORGAN, AL. *The Great Man.* New York: E. P. Dutton & Co., Inc., 1955.

NIEBUHR, H. RICHARD. *The Meaning of Revelation.* New York: The Macmillan Company, 1941.

NIEBUHR, REINHOLD, *Beyond Tragedy.* London: Nisbet and Co., Ltd., 1947.

———. *The Self and the Dramas of History.* New York: Charles Scribner's Sons, 1955.

PARKER, EVERETT C., BARRY, DAVID W., and SMYTHE, DALLAS W. *The Television-Radio Audience and Religion.* New York: Harper & Brothers, 1955.

PERRIN, HENRI. *Priest-Workman in Germany.* Trans. Rosemary Sheed. London: Sheed & Ward, 1948.

PITTENGER, W. NORMAN. *Christ In The Haunted Wood.* Greenwich: The Seabury Press, Inc., 1953.

POWDERMAKER, HORTENSE. *Hollywood the Dream Factory.* Boston: Little, Brown & Company, 1950.

READ, DAVID H. C. *The Communication of the Gospel.* London: SCM Press Ltd., 1952.

RIESMAN, DAVID. *The Lonely Crowd.* New Haven: Yale University Press, 1950.

ROSS, LILLIAN. *Picture.* New York: Rinehart & Company, Inc., 1952.

SAYERS, DOROTHY L. *The Man Born To Be King.* London: Victor Gollancz, Ltd., 1943.

SCHARY, DORE. *Case History of a Movie.* New York: Random House, 1950.

———. "Creative Responsibility." Address delivered before Advertising Association of the West, Statler Hotel, Los Angeles, June 27, 1956.

SCHRAMM, WILBUR (ed.) *The Process and Effects of Mass Communication.* Urbana: University of Illinois Press, 1954.

SCHULBERG, BUDD. *The Disenchanted.* New York: Random House, 1950.

———. *What Makes Sammy Run?* Garden City: The Sun Dial Press, 1943.

SELDES, GILBERT. *The Great Audience.* New York: The Viking Press, Inc., 1950.

———. *The Public Arts.* New York: Simon and Schuster, Inc., 1956.

SOUTHCOTT, ERNEST. *Receive This Child.* London: A. R. Mowbray & Company, Ltd., 1951.

———. *The Parish Comes Alive.* New York: Morehouse-Gorham, 1957.

SPECTORSKY, A. C. *The Exurbanites.* Philadelphia J. B. Lippincott Company, 1955.

SPROXTON, VERNON. *Watching Films.* London: SCM Press Ltd., 1948.

TAVARD, GEORGE H. *The Catholic Approach to Protestantism.* New York: Harper & Brothers, 1955.

TEMPLE, WILLIAM. *Christianity and Social Order.* London: SCM Press Ltd., 1950.

TILLICH, PAUL. *Systematic Theology, Vol. I.* Chicago: University of Chicago Press, 1951.

UNDERWOOD, AGNESS. *Newspaperwoman.* New York: Harper & Brothers, 1949.

VIDLER, ALEC. *The Theology of F. D. Maurice.* London: SCM Press Ltd., 1948.

WEST, NATHANIEL. *The Day of the Locust,* Norfolk, Conn.: New Directions, 1939.

WILDER, AMOS N. *Modern Poetry and the Christian Tradition: A Study in the Relation of Christianity to Culture.* New York: Charles Scribner's Sons, 1952.

WOLF, HANS (ed.). *Motivation Research, A New Aid to Understanding Your Market.* Boston: Motivation Research Associates, 1955.

PERIODICALS AND NEWSPAPERS

BOYD, MALCOLM. "All Films Are Theological." *The Christian Century,* 71:1456–57, Dec. 1, 1954.

———. "Christians On The Assembly-Line." *Episcopal Churchnews,* 120:26, 32–33, September 4, 1955.

———. "Comics With A Goal." *Episcopal Churchnews,* 120:16–17, Dec. 11, 1955.

———. "Communicating As Christians." *Religion In Life,* Vol. 26, winter, 1956.

———. "Crisis in Communications." *Episcopal Churchnews,* 119:24, 34–36, August 8, 1954.

———. "The Crisis of the Mass Media." *Christianity and Crisis,* 16: 69–72, May 28, 1956.

———. "House-Church: Visual." *Episcopal Churchnews,* 120:28, Feb. 6, 1955.

———. "The Industrial Mission." *Episcopal Churchnews,* 120:27, 30–32, March 6, 1955.

———. "New Ways To Communicate." *The Christian Century,* 73: 270–71, Feb. 29, 1956.

———. "O Ye Radio, Press and Television, Bless Ye The Lord." *Episcopal Churchnews,* 120:28–29, 36, Feb. 21, 1954.

———. "Parish Fellowship and The House-Church." *Episcopal Churchnews,* 120:21, Jan. 23, 1955.

———. "Point of Contact." *Anglican Theological Review,* Vol. 39, No. 1: Jan. 1957.

———. "Religious Programming." *Variety,* 193:97, Jan. 6, 1954.

———. "Theology in Films." *The Hollywood Reporter,* 23d Anniversary Issue, Oct. 26, 1953.

———. "The Web and the Cross." *Union Seminary Quarterly Review,* Vol. 12, January 1957.

"Christians, Jews Group Says It Believes In Advertising; Symposium Views Not Its Own." *Advertising Age,* 26: 2, 6, November 21, 1955.

CLENDENEN, RICHARD AND BEASER, HERBERT W. "The Shame of America." *The Saturday Evening Post,* 227:85, January 22, 1955.

DESICA, VITTORIO. "Analyzing 'Umberto.'" New York *Times,* October 30, 1955, p. X5.

Film Daily, 109:6, March 6, 1956.

GORDON, ERNEST. "I Beheld His Glory." *Theology,* 57:46, February, 1954.

GOULD, JACK. "On Faith Healing." New York *Times,* Feb. 19, 1956, p. X9.

GRAHAM, BILLY. "Billy Graham Answers His Critics." *Look,* 20:47, February 7, 1956.

HARVEY, VAN A. "Pageantry and Relics." *Episcopal Churchnews,* 120:26, March 6, 1955.

HOTCHKISS, JOHN. "The Battle for Men's Minds." *The New Statesman and Nation,* 48:380, October 2, 1954.

"In Review." *Broadcasting-Telecasting,* 49:14, August 22, 1955.

International News Service dispatch, Los Angeles *Herald-Express,* September 5, 1952, p. 1.

"Jack Mabley Launches Anti-Crime Crusade." *TV,* 6:3, January, 1953.

JARRETT-KERR, MARTIN, C. R. "A Saint On The Threshold." *The Frontier,* 2:30, January, 1951.

"Madam Ambassador Clare Booth Luce: Her Versatile and Crowded Years." *Newsweek,* 45:28, January 24, 1955.

MAURY, PIERRE. "Evangelism—The Mission of the Church to Those Outside Her Life." *The Ecumenical Review,* 7:29–35, October, 1954.

MILLER, WILLIAM LEE. "On Giving the Public What it Wants." *Episcopal Churchnews,* Jan. 10, 1954.

———. "It May be Box Office, But is it the Bible?" *The Reporter,* September 29, 1953.

———. "The Problem of Mass Communication." *Religious Education,* November–December, 1954.

"Oceans of Empathy." *Time,* 55:72–78, February 27, 1950.

ORME, FRANK. "The Television Code." *The Quarterly of Film, Radio and Television,* published by the University of California Press, 6:404–413, Summer, 1952.

PRIESTLEY, J. B. "The World of the Novel—Cops & Robbers." London *Sunday Times,* November 21, 1954.

"Profile—Billy Graham." *The Observer* (London), April 24, 1955, p. 3.

Radio Daily, 69:1, March 2, 1955.

RAMSDELL, EDWARD T. "Communications From a Christian Perspective." *Religious Education,* 50:335–9, Sept.-Oct., 1955.

"Review of *Day of Triumph.*" *The Hollywood Reporter,* 132:4, December 1, 1954.

"Review of *The Sign of The Cross.*" *Variety,* Vol. 108:14, December 6, 1932.

SCHWARTZ, DELMORE. "The Starlight's Intuition Pierced the Twelve." *The Kenyon Review,* 11:383–5, Summer, 1944.

SHERWOOD, R. E. "Review of *Ben Hur.*" Literary Digest, 88:29, February 6, 1926.

SMYTHE, DALLAS W. "Some Observations on Communication Theory." *Audio-Visual Communication Review,* Vol. 2, p. 24.

SOUTHCOTT, ERNEST. "The House Church." *Christian News-Letter,* 2 (New Series): 124, July, 1954.

STRYKER, PERRIN. "Motivation Research." *Fortune* 103:144–232. June, 1956.

"The Christian Frontier." *The Frontier,* 1:32–8, January, *The Moving Picture World,* 14:233, October 19, 1912.

"The New Evangelist." *Time,* 64:38, October 25, 1954.

TILLICH, PAUL. "Communicating the Gospel." *Union Seminary Quarterly Review,* 7:3–11, June, 1952.

"Too Concrete?" *Time,* 52:87, October 11, 1948.

WEDEL, THEODORE O. "Group Dynamics and the Church." *Theology Today,* 10:511–24, January, 1954.

WHITESIDE, THOMAS. "The Communicator." (I.—Athens Starts Pouring In), *The New Yorker,* 30:38, October 16, 1954.

WICKHAM, E. R. "The Sheffield Industrial Mission." *Christian News-Letter,* 3 (New Series): 33, January, 1955.

WISEMAN, THOMAS. "Mr. Mature Is Just A Trifle Nervous." London *Evening Standard,* June 18, 1955, p. 6.